ROME

*The Timeless Guide to
the Eternal City*

VESNA NESKOW

ILLUSTRATED BY
KERREN BARBAS STECKLER

PETER PAUPER PRESS, INC.
WHITE PLAINS, NEW YORK

FOR MY SISTER ELIZABETH,
A GREAT TRAVEL COMPANION

Editor: Mara Conlon
Designed by Heather Zschock
Illustrations copyright © 2014 Kerren Barbas Steckler
Rome Transportation map © 2014 Communicarta Ltd.
Neighborhood maps © 2014 David Lindroth Inc.

Copyright © 2014
Peter Pauper Press, Inc.
202 Mamaroneck Avenue
White Plains, NY 10601
All rights reserved
ISBN 978-1-4413-1356-0
Printed in Hong Kong
7 6 5 4 3 2 1

The publisher has made every effort to ensure that the content of this book was current at time of publication. It's always best, however, to confirm information before making final travel plans, since telephone numbers, Web sites, prices, hours of operation, and other facts are always subject to change. The publisher cannot accept responsibility for any consequences arising from the use of this book. We value your feedback and suggestions. Please write to: Editors, Peter Pauper Press, Inc., 202 Mamaroneck Avenue, Suite 400, White Plains, New York 10601-5376.

Visit us at www.peterpauper.com

THE LITTLE
BLACK BOOK OF
ROME

CONTENTS

INTRODUCTION 6
- *How to Use This Guide* 9
- *All About Money* 11
- *Public Transportation* 12
- *Making Phone Calls* 15
- *Meals* 15
- *Shopping* 15
- *Say It in Italian* 17
- *Etiquette Tips* 19
- *On the Town: Plays, Concerts, Events, Exhibits* 19
- *Tourist Information* 21
- *Seasonal Events* 22
- *Rome's Top Picks* 27

CHAPTER 1 28
- *Piazza Navona* 31
- *Pantheon* 40
- *Campo dei Fiori/Ghetto* 46

CHAPTER 2 54
- *Tridente/Piazza di Spagna* 57
- *Via Veneto* 65
- *Villa Borghese* 70

CHAPTER 3 74
- *Quirinale/Trevi* 77
- *Esquilino & Monti* 84

San Lorenzo *90*

CHAPTER 4 . . . . *94*
   Lateran *97*
   Celio *102*
   Caracalla *110*
   Outskirts off Caracalla *115*

CHAPTER 5 . . . . *116*
   Capitoline/Campidoglio *119*
   Forum & Colosseum *126*
   Palatine *135*

CHAPTER 6 . . . . *140*
   Aventine *143*
   Testaccio *151*
   Ostiense *157*

CHAPTER 7 . . . . *160*
   Trastevere *163*
   Gianicolo *175*

CHAPTER 8 . . . . *182*
   Vatican & Borgo *184*
   Prati *194*

INDEX *201*

NOTES *212*

TRANSPORTATION MAP *221*

INTRODUCTION

Rome, the Eternal City. Its epithet says it all: history and modernity play equal parts in making Rome timeless, magical. More than 2,700 years of numerous civilizations coexist side by side or piled on top of each other. Founded in 753 BC, the Iron Age village became the most sophisticated city of Europe—first through a short

Etruscan period, then with the birth of the Republic and the powerful Roman Empire, which expanded its boundaries of influence throughout Europe and North Africa. But the Romans were neither the first nor the last—perhaps only the most spectacular—to teach us that power breeds corruption, greed, and decadence. Democracy gave way to dictatorship and eventually Rome declined as an empire, leaving the control of the city to a medieval clergy whose lust for power was hardly hidden. Luckily, the Middle Ages were followed by the Renaissance and the Baroque eras, and Rome flourished with great art and architecture for several centuries. In 1870, adjoining city-states were unified and Italy came into being with Rome as its capital.

Today, that rich history has made Rome a living museum. The best way by far to see Rome is to wander through its streets. Stumble across its splendors. Turn the corner and let yourself be awed by a sumptuous fountain, a Bernini sculpture, a  Baroque obelisk, or an ancient arch. Or maybe a diminutive Madonna, sculpted into the corner of an ochre-colored building, seeming to watch over you as your feet take your heart on a tour of discovery. Splendor, drama, and romance are all built right into the city. It's voluptuous and it's erotic. Rome is glorious—and it's all on show.

Rome isn't just a museum, however. Its citizens wear their history with pride but live in the present. The city pulses with new technology, and the latest in art, architecture, fashion, and culinary wizardry bring modern pilgrims to the City of the Seven Hills. Ultra-modern architecture, such as the Auditorium-Parco della Musica, places Rome squarely among the leading cities shaping the vision and form of the 21st-century metropolis.

Yet Romans themselves accept change with a shrug of the shoulders. They like their city's reputation as *Caput Mundi*, but being *Head of the World* should not mean giving up their leisurely pace of life, taking pleasure in the daily rituals that give substance to existence. When Fellini made *La Dolce Vita*, it wasn't by chance that he shot the film in Rome, where "the sweet life" is the only way to live. To this day, Romans still close shop at least an hour for lunch. They meet neighbors at local bars and greet acquaintances during the evening stroll along the Via del Corso. The piazza—the city square—is truly a meeting place: governments may fall, film stars may scandalize, globalization may transform old-fashioned businesses, but Romans continue to fill the piazza, interacting and expressing themselves as exuberantly and as warmly today as they did millennia ago. The fascination of Rome is as much in its people as in its places and objects.

This guidebook is meant to assist you in discovering that allure. All the splendors of Rome are too numerous to include in any one book; this one will introduce you to some of its highlights to help you embark on your exploration of this magical city. As you discover Rome, you will also discover yourself. It's a journey of love. After all, as any Roman will tell you with delight, *Roma* (the Italian for "Rome") is *Amor* spelled backwards. So let *Love* be your guide as you tuck this book into your pocket and set foot onto cobblestones that have been trod by Julius Caesar, Agrippina, Michelangelo,

Artemisia Gentileschi, Galileo, Pier Paolo Pasolini, and Renzo Piano. The genius and grandeur of the Eternal City will surely touch your spirit.

HOW TO USE THIS GUIDE

Each chapter is divided into clusters of neighborhoods. A fold-out map is included for each chapter with color-coded numbers corresponding to the places mentioned in the text. **Red** symbols indicate **Places to See** (landmarks and arts & entertainment). **Blue** symbols indicate **Places to Eat & Drink** (restaurants, cafés, bars, and nightlife). **Orange** symbols indicate **Where to Shop**. **Green** symbols indicate **Where to Stay**. Some shops and restaurants are closed in July and August, so check before going. Each place mentioned is followed by its address, local telephone number, Web site, and hours, if available.

Here are our keys for restaurant and hotel costs:

Restaurants
Cost of an appetizer and main course without drinks

(€)	Up to €25
(€€)	€25-€50
(€€€)	€50-€75
(€€€€)	€75 and up

Hotels
Cost per room per night

(€)	Up to €150
(€€)	€150-€250
(€€€)	€250-€400
(€€€€)	€400 and up

Abbreviations

B	bus line
M	metropolitana (subway) station
P.za	piazza (square)

ALL ABOUT MONEY

Money changing

The currency in Italy is euros (€). Most places accept credit cards. For cash withdrawals in euros, ATMs *(bancomat)* offer good exchange rates. (Contact your bank before leaving home to determine if you need an international PIN for your cash card or credit cards.) Exchange rates for cash or travelers' checks are best in banks (usually open Monday–Friday, 8:30AM–4PM, closed for lunch), bad at the many independent exchange bureaux *(cambio)*, and worst at hotels and shops. You can also change money and get tourist information at **American Express** (*P.za di Spagna 38, 06-6764.2250; hours: M–F 9AM–5:30PM, Sa 9AM–12:30PM*).

Cash or credit?

Cash is generally preferred by Roman businesses. Many stores and eateries will request (or even require) that you pay in cash. Some shopkeepers may give you a discount for doing so, and restaurants will often waive their "seating fee." As such, it's advisable to carry enough money to cover most of the spending you plan to do during the day. In a pinch, most business owners can direct you to the nearest ATM.

Tipping

Tipping is a gray area, but don't look to Italians: foreigners should tip more than locals. If a service charge isn't included in your restaurant bill, a 10% tip is generally appropriate; if it's included, leave small change. At casual places, €1 to €5 is OK. For drinks at bar counters, leave small change. For taxis, round up the fare. Leave housekeeping and bellboys €1 or €2; the concierge, €2 or €3. Theater ushers are tipped at least 50¢.

euro-sense

Decimal points and commas are reversed from the U.S. system. So euros are separated from euro-cents *(centesimi)* by a comma, and hundreds are separated from thousands by a period (e.g., €2.425,50).

PUBLIC TRANSPORTATION

Getting to and from the Airport

Rome has two major airports: Leonardo da Vinci–Fiumicino *(colloquially, "Fiumicino," after the town where it is located, 06-65.951, www.adr.it)* and Ciampino *(06-65.951, www.adr.it)*, which services mostly charter flights. Flights from the U.S. would go to Fiumicino. A taxi from Fiumicino to Rome costs at least €40. Book a taxi through Airport Connection Services *(06-338.32.21, www.airportconnection.it)* or P.I.T. inside the airport *(Tourist Information Point of Rome)*.

An **express train service** goes from Fiumicino to Rome's main train station, Stazione Termini, every 30 minutes from about 6AM to about 11PM. It takes 31 minutes and costs €14. The **regular train service** goes to Trastevere, Ostiense, Tuscolana, and Tiburtina stations; it takes 25 to 40 minutes and costs €8. Tickets can be purchased in the airport lobby or train stations. Before boarding you must stamp your ticket in the machines on the train station platform.

Terravision **coaches** *(06-9761.0632, www.terravision.eu)* run between Fiumicino and Termini *(opposite Royal Santina Hotel, Via Marsala 22, 06-9784.3383; hours: M–Su 8AM–8PM)* every two hours during the day. They take 70 minutes and cost €6, online €4 one way. **Night buses** run every hour or so between Fiumicino–Termini–Tiburtina and cost €5 one way. The train stations are a bit unsafe at night (and known havens for pickpockets), so it's best to take a taxi there and back.

Metro & Bus Tickets

The city transport system *(run by ATAC, www.atac.roma.it)* consists of buses, trams, and metro (subway). There are only two metro lines, so buses are usually the better bet. You will find a public transportation map in the back of this book. We've introduced each section with a listing of several different bus routes you can use to get to the neighborhood (and metro information, if applicable). Within the center of the city, walking is your best means of transport.

You can buy tickets at newspaper kiosks, tobacconist shops *(tabacchi)*, or metro stations. You must validate your ticket at the beginning of your trip by punching it in one of the machines on the bus or at the metro station. A BIT ticket, for unlimited bus trips and one metro trip, is valid for 100 minutes and costs €1,5. A one-day BIG ticket gets you anywhere in Rome for €6.

e-day BTI pass, €16.50, covers city buses, metro, ns to Ostia (second class). The weekly CIS pass 4.

Taxis
Taxis are best requested by phone *(06-35.70; 06-49.94; 06-66.45; 06-88.22)*. Expect extra charges for luggage, night fares, and rides outside the city. Round up your fare to include a small tip.

Bus and Boat Tours
Combined bus and boat tours come with audio guides (€32–€40). Dinner tours down the Tiber (€58) are also available. Tickets can be purchased from Battelli di Roma *(06-9774.5414, www.battellidiroma.it)* at the jetty or online.

Bike/Scooter/Moped Rentals
It might be daunting to join Roman drivers on the streets, but bikes, scooters, and mopeds are convenient for getting around parks and more distant areas. Here are some places that rent such vehicles, by district:

VIA VENETO: Scooters for Rent *(bikes, mopeds)*, Via della Purificazione 84, 06-488.54.85, *www.travel.it/roma/scooters*

CAMPO DEI FIORI/GHETTO: Collatti *(bikes)*, Via del Pellegrino 82, 06-68.80.10.84; RomaRent *(bikes, scooters, mopeds, bike tours)*, Vicolo dei Bovari 7A, 06-689.65.55, *web.tiscali.it/romarent*

ESQUILINO/MONTI: Happy Rent *(scooters, mopeds)*, Via di San Martino ai Monti 9, 06-488.42.15, *www.happyrent.com*; Treno e Scooter Rent *(bikes, scooters, mopeds)*, Termini Station, 06-4890.5823, *www.trenoescooter.com*; Scoot-a-Long *(scooters, mopeds)*, Via Cavour 302, 06-678.02.06

MAKING PHONE CALLS

The area code for Rome is 06. When dialing within Italy or Rome, dial the number as it appears, including the 06 area code for Rome. Italian 800 area codes are toll-free. Note: phone numbers in Rome consist of the area code plus 5, 6, 7, or 8 digits. To make an international call from Rome, dial 00 plus country code (1 for U.S.), area code, and number. When calling Rome direct from the U.S., dial 011-39, then the full number.

MEALS

In Italy, pasta is a course, not a meal. The main courses are: *antipasto* (appetizer), *primo* (small pasta portion), and *secondo* (entrée). It's usual in Italy to eat a *primo* and *secondo*. And don't forget the *dolci* (desserts)!

SHOPPING

Hours: Shop hours are generally 9AM–1PM and 3:30PM–7:30PM (4PM–8PM in summer). Some shops stay open from 10AM–7:30PM. Many shops close during the lunch hours, from 2PM–4PM or 1PM–3:30PM. *Chiuso per Ferie* means the shop is closed for vacation, mostly in

August, sometimes July. Most shops are closed on Sundays and in the summer on Saturday afternoons (Monday mornings in winter).

Sales: Sales *(saldi)* are held twice a year, mid-January through February, and mid-July through mid-September. Otherwise, good deals are marked in stores as "*promozioni.*"

Tax Refunds: In stores with a "Europe Tax Free" or "Global Refund" sticker, non-EU citizens can get a refund for part of the sales tax if you spend a minimum of €155 in that store on one day. You must show your passport and you'll be given a form in the store. When leaving Italy, go to the customs office at the airport and have your form stamped (Global Refund Office, Fiumicino Airport, Terminals B and C). You'll have to show your passport and store receipt. You may have to show your purchases, so it's best to do this before check-in, or else keep your purchases in your carry-on. Once home, return one copy of the form in the envelope provided and keep the other copy for yourself. You must do this within 90 days of the purchase.

If traveling to other EU countries, get your forms stamped in the airport customs office of the last EU country you leave. It takes about three months to get the refund. You might be able to get your refund at a Global Refund office in Rome by the Spanish Steps at P.za Trinità dei Monti 17/A.

Department Stores: La Rinascente and Coin are Italy's largest chain department stores, with outlets throughout Rome. Upim is a chain discount store.

SAY IT IN ITALIAN

A phrase book is always good to have on hand, but you might want to learn some basic words and phrases.

Parla inglese? *(PAR-lah een-GLAY-zeh)* Do you speak English?
Buon giorno *(boo-ohn GEOR-no)* Good morning (before lunch)
Buona sera *(boo-ohma SEHR-ah)* Good afternoon/evening (after lunch)
Buona notte *(boo-ohna NOH-tay)* Good night
Arrivederci *(ah-ree-veh-DEHR-chee)* Good-bye
Ciao *(CHOW)* Hi/'Bye
Per favore *(pair fah-VOH-reh)* Please
Vorrei *(voh-RAY)* I'd like
Grazie *(GRAH-tsee-yay)* Thank you
Prego *(PREY-go)* You're welcome
Permesso *(pair-MESS-oh)* Excuse me (to move past someone in a crowd)
Mi scusi *(me SCOO-zee)* Excuse me (to get attention; sorry)
Mi dispiace *(me dees-pee-YA-cheh)* I'm sorry
Va bene *(vah BEH-neh)* OK/That's OK
Aspetta *(ahss-PET-ah)* Wait
Andiamo *(ahn-dee-YA-moh)* Let's go
Si *(SEE)* Yes
No *(NOH)* No
Dov'è… *(doh-VEH)* Where is…
la metropolitana *(la metro-polee-TAH-na)* subway
metro *(met-ROH)* subway (short version)
un biglietto *(oon bee-LEEYE-toh)* a ticket

la strada *(la STRAH-da)* the street
Via *(VEE-yah)* street (name)
l'albergo *(l'ahl-BEAR-goh)* hotel
il negozio *(il neh-GOH-tsee-oh)* store
il ristorante *(il ree-stoh-RAHN-teh)* restaurant
il palazzo *(il pah-LAH-tsoh)* apartment building; palace; mansion
la piazza *(la pee-AH-tsah)* square (town square)
Dove sono i gabinetti? *(DOH-veh SOH-noh ee gab-ee-NET-ee)* Where is the bathroom?
Quanto costa? *(KWAN-toh COST-ah)* How much does it cost?
Signora *(see-NYO-rah)* Ma'am, Mrs.
Signorina *(see-nyo-REE-nah)* Miss
Signor/Signore *(see-NYO-reh)* Sir, Mr.
cameriere *(kahm-air-ee-AIR-eh)* waiter
cameriera *(kahm-ahr-ee-AIR-ah)* waitress
chi *(KEE)* who
cosa *(KOH-ZA)* what
Cos'è? *(koz-EH)* What is it?
dove *(DOH-veh)* where
come *(KOH-meh)* how
quanti *(KWAHN-tee)* many, how many
quanto *(KWAHN-toh)* much, how much
quando *(KWAHN-doh)* when
colazione *(koh-lah-tsee-OH-neh)* breakfast
pranzo *(PRAHN-tsoh)* lunch
cena *(CHEH-na)* dinner

ETIQUETTE TIPS

When entering a shop always say, "Buon giorno" ("Good morning"—before lunch) or "Buona sera" ("Good afternoon"—after lunch). Before handling merchandise, ask, "Posso?" (May I?).

It's more polite to add "Signore" or "Signora" when greeting someone—though just saying "Buon giorno" or "Buona sera" without the title is not rude.

To get the attention of a waiter, call out "Senta!" (literally, "Listen!") or "Scusi!" ("Excuse me").

ON THE TOWN: PLAYS, CONCERTS, EVENTS, EXHIBITS

BOOKING TICKETS: Tickets for theater and classical concerts are usually purchased at the theater. Tickets for rock, jazz, and classical concerts as well as certain sports events can also be obtained at the **Feltrinelli** music store's "Box Office" *(Via del Corso 506, 06-361.23.70; hours: daily 9AM–10PM)* and at **Orbis** *(P.za del Esquilino 37, 06-482.74.03)*.

LISTINGS: Listings magazines for arts, entertainment, and other events include *L'Evento* (available at APT—*see page 21*), the weekly magazine *Roma c'è* (with an English "Week in Rome" section), and *Trovaroma*, a supplement to the Thursday edition of the newspaper *La Repubblica*.

FREE CONCERTS: Tourist info booths offer pamphlets listing free concerts *(see page 21)*. Churches and foreign institutes give free concerts. The latter include the Belgian Academy *(Via Omero 8, 06-2039.8631, www.academiabelgica.it)*, the Austrian Cultural Institute *(Viale Bruno Buozzi 113, 06-360.83.71)*, the Japanese Cultural Institute *(Via Gramsci 74, 06-322.47.94, www.jpf.go.jp)*, and the Hungarian Academy *(Via Giulia 1, 06-688.96.71)*. The Music Festival sponsors all sorts of free concerts around the city every June 21st.

PARCO DELLA MUSICA *(Viale Pietro de Coubertin 30, 06-80.24.12.81, www.auditorium.com, B: 53, 910)*, less than two miles north of Piazza del Popolo, is Rome's premier auditorium for classical music.

MACRO *(Via Nizza 138, 06-67.10.70.400, 06-06.08, www.museomacro.org; hours: Tu–F, Su 11AM–7PM, til 9PM for public spaces, Sa 11AM–10PM, B: 36, 60, 84, 90)*, the Museum for Contemporary Art of Rome, is an exciting center featuring Italian art since the 1960s.

MAXXI *(Via Guido Reni 4A, 06-3996.7350, www.fondazionemaxxi.it; hours: Tu–F, Su 11AM–7PM, Sa 11AM–10PM, B: 19, 53, 217, 225, 910)*, the National Museum of 21st-Century Art, is an exhibition and performance space. At the time of this publication it was still in the construction phase; however, temporary exhibits are being held in a nearby hangar.

FORO ITALICO—Sports Arenas *(P.za L. de Bosis/Via del Foro Italico, B: 32, 224, 280)* is where Rome's major-league soccer teams, AS Roma *(www.asroma.it)* and SS

Lazio *(www.sslazio.it),* compete. The Italian Open is held at the nearby tennis courts *(see Seasonal Events, page 23).*

TOURIST INFORMATION

Web sites: Several sites give helpful general information and updates on exhibitions, events, festivals, bars, nightclubs, etc. These include:

www.italiantourism.com
www.comune.roma.it/cultura
www.romaturismo.it
www.capitolium.org
www.romainweb.com (Italian only)

Italian Tourist Offices in the U.S.:
NY: 212-245-5618
LA: 310-820-1898
CHI: 312-644-0996

Tourist Offices in Rome:
The **APT** (Azienda di Promozione Turistica) gives information, free brochures, and free city maps.

APT in Rome: Via Parigi 11, Esquilino, 06-48.89.91; hours: M–Sa 9AM–7PM
APT at Fiumicino Airport: Terminal 3; hours: daily 8AM–7:30PM

Information kiosks around the city:
Termini Station: Platform 2 (06-48.90.63.00)
Fori Imperiali: Piazza Tempio della Pace (06-69.92.43.07)

Piazza di Spagna: Largo Goldoni (06-06.08)
Piazza Navona: Piazza Cinque Lune (06-68.80.92.40)
Via Nazionale: Palazzo delle Esposizioni (06-47.82.45.25)
Trastevere: Piazza Sonnino (06-58.33.34.57)
San Giovanni: Piazza di San Giovanni in Laterano (06-06.08)
Castel Sant'Angelo: Piazza Pia (06-68.80.97.07)

SEASONAL EVENTS

Romans will do anything for a party, and just about any saint's day is reason enough to hold a festival. The weather sometimes inspires all-night bashes. Spring and autumn are the best seasons in Rome. Winter tends to be rainy, while summer is very hot. Most Romans leave the city in August and often in July as well.

Spring:

Rome Marathon (3rd or 4th Sunday in March)—on city streets, begins and ends on Via dei Fori Imperiali *(Maratona di Roma, 06-406.50.64, www.maratonadiroma.it)*.

Easter (March/April)—Holy Week is marked by services throughout Rome and open-air masses at St. Peter's Square; the pope leads the Stations of the Cross and mass on Good Friday *(Colosseum, late evening)* and addresses the people gathered in St. Peter's Square on Easter Sunday *(P.za San Pietro, Vatican)*.

Rome's Birthday—April 21 (or preceding Sunday)—Fireworks at Piazza del Campidoglio mark the founding of Rome in 753 BC.

Via Margutta Art Fair (4–5 days, April–May, also October–November)—Art galleries on a charming street once full of artists' studios open their doors *(Via Margutta, 06-812.33.40, www.centopittoriviamargutta.it)*.

Settimana della Cultura—Culture Week (April/May)—Many museums, archaeological sites, and cultural centers offer free admission; some normally restricted archives open their doors to the public; and special artistic and cultural events take place *(06-6723.2635/2390/2851, www.beniculturali.it)*.

International Horse Show (late April–early May)—The world's elite equestrians gather for this prestigious show-jumping event. *(P.za di Siena, Villa Borghese, 06-836.6841, www.fise.it)*.

May Day—Primo Maggio (May 1)—A free rock concert sponsored by labor unions; it marks International Workers' Day *(P.za di San Giovanni in Laterano)*.

Italian Open Tennis Tournament (2 weeks, early May)—An international tennis event *(Foro Italico, Viale dei Gladiatori 31, northern outskirts, 800-622.662, it.internazional ibnlditalia.com)*.

Summer:

Festival Internazionale delle Letterature (May–June)—In an ancient setting, renowned writers from around the world read from their work *(Basilica di Massenzio, enter at Clivo di Venere Felice in Via dei Fori Imperiali, 06-06.08, www.festivaldelleletterature.it; hours: daily 9AM–9PM)*.

Estate Romana (Roman Summer) (June–September)—A popular festival featuring plays, dance, concerts, opera, and films, all in outdoor venues, many free *(check local press listings, www.estateromana.it)*.

Political Party Festivals (June–September)—Free open-air events, street fairs, concerts, and performances are organized by political parties. These are family-oriented events and everyone goes, regardless of political affiliation; the biggest is Festa dell'Unità, the Communists' bash *(various venues, check listings)*.

Isola del Cinema (June–August)—Indie film festival held in an open-air cinema on Tiber Island spotlights emerging directors. Bars and restaurants help make it more than a night at the movies *(Isola Tiberina, 06-5833.3113, www.isoladelcinema.com)*.

Alta Roma Fashion Week (July; January)—Designers present their new lines in historical venues; though by invitation only, you can squeeze in the back or find an elevated spot from which to peek at the drama of high fashion *(check local listings)*.

Festa dei Noantri (last 2 weeks of July)—Trastevere celebrates its working-class origins with an open-air carnival, replete with music, performances, street fairs, and fireworks *(P.za Santa Maria in Trastevere, P.za Mastai)*.

Ferragosto (Feast of the Assumption) (August 15)—Those who've stayed in the city take a long weekend for this holy day, and Rome practically closes down—a good time to go to the beach.

Autumn:

Enzimi (September, 2 weeks)—The cutting edge in creative talent debuts at this free festival of the arts. Theatre, dance, and music events *(various venues)* are especially interesting.

RomaEuropa Festival (September–November)—This very cool performing arts festival brings together avant-garde and classical dance, theater, and music *(various venues, 06-4555.3050, www.romaeuropa.net)*.

Via Margutta Art Fair (4–5 days, October–November) *(see page 23, Spring)*.

Winter:

Christmas (December 24–25)—The pope celebrates midnight mass on Christmas Eve *(St. Peter's Basilica, Vatican; for tickets, fax the Prefect of the Papal Household, 06-69.88.58.63, www.vatican.va)* and blesses the crowds in St. Peter's Square on Christmas Day *(noon, Vatican)*.

New Year's (December 31–January 1)—Fireworks and a free concert in Piazza del Popolo on New Year's Eve are brilliant and fairly raucous. Check out the crazy river divers, who plunge into the Tiber from the Cavour Bridge on New Year's Day.

Alta Roma Fashion Week (January) *(see page 24, Summer).*

ROME'S TOP PICKS

TOP PICK!

Rome offers an abundance of one-of-a-kind attractions and experiences for visitors. Here are 13 of the top picks not to be missed!

- ★ **Piazza Navona** *(see page 32)*
- ★ **National Museum of Rome—Palazzo Altemps** *(see page 34)*
- ★ **Pantheon** *(see page 40)*
- ★ **Spanish Steps** *(see page 59)*
- ★ **Villa Borghese/Galleria Borghese** *(see page 71)*
- ★ **Trevi Fountain** *(see page 78)*
- ★ **Santa Maria Maggiore** *(see page 85)*
- ★ **San Pietro in Vincoli** *(see page 85)*
- ★ **Baths of Caracalla** *(see page 112)*
- ★ **Capitoline Museums** *(see page 123)*
- ★ **Roman Forum/Colosseum** *(see pages 126-134)*
- ★ **St. Peter's Basilica** *(see pages 186-188)*
- ★ **Raphael Rooms/Sistine Chapel** *(see page 190)*

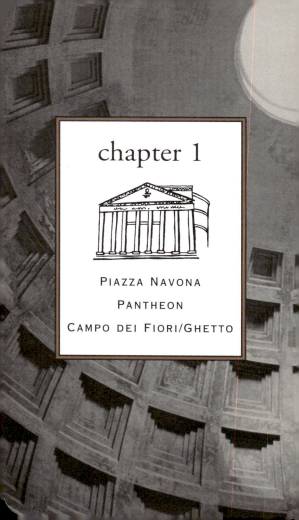

chapter 1

PIAZZA NAVONA
PANTHEON
CAMPO DEI FIORI/GHETTO

Piazza Navona
Pantheon
Campo dei Fiori/Ghetto

Places to See:
1. PIAZZA NAVONA ★
2. Fountain of the Four Rivers
3. Sant'Agnese in Agone
4. Santa Maria della Pace
5. Chiesa Nuova
6. Pasquino
7. Palazzo Madama
8. San Luigi dei Francesi
9. Museum of Rome
10. NATIONAL MUSEUM OF ROME—PALAZZO ALTEMPS ★
11. Teatro Valle
32. PANTHEON ★
33. Santa Maria sopra Minerva
34. Gesù
35. Temple of Hadrian
36. Column of Marcus Aurelius
37. Galleria Alberto Sordi
38. Palazzo Doria Pamphilj
54. Campo dei Fiori
55. Palazzo Farnese
56. Palazzo Spada
57. Galleria Spada
58. Sant'Andrea della Valle
59. Largo Argentina Sacred Precincts
60. Crypta Balbi
61. Fountain of the Tortoises
62. Via Giulia
63. Portico d'Ottavia
64. Theatre of Marcellus
65. Synagogue
66. Museum of Jewish Culture
67. Isola Tiberina
68. Ponte Rotto
69. Piccola Farnesina
70. Teatro Argentina

Places to Eat & Drink:
12. Hostaria dell'Orso
13. Santa Lucia
14. Antica Biblioteca
15. Da Baffetto
16. Raphaël
17. Bloom
18. Via della Pace
19. Bar della Pace
20. La Maison
21. Casa Bleve
39. Maccheroni
40. Osteria dell'Ingegno
41. Caffè Sant'Eustachio
42. Tazza d'Oro
43. La Rosetta

★ *Top Picks*

44. Habana Café
71. Taverna Giulia
72. Assunta Madre
73. Al Bric
74. Bar Farnese
75. Al Pompiere
76. Piperno
77. La Vineria

Where to Shop:
22. Via dei Coronari
23. Via del Governo Vecchio
24. Josephine de Huertas & Co.
25. Luna & L'Altra
26. Vestiti Usati Cinzia
45. Degli Effetti
46. Magazzino d'Arte Moderna
47. Art'è
48. Confetteria Moriondo e Gariglio
78. Via del Pellegrino
79. Via dei Cappellari

80. Mondello Ottica
81. Borini
82. Il museo del Louvre
88. Ilaria Miani

Where to Stay:
27. Hotel Due Torri
28. Hotel Portoghesi
29. Residenza Zanardelli
30. Hotel Navona
31. Raphaël
49. Relais al Senato
50. Albergo Santa Chiara
51. Sole al Pantheon
52. Grand Hotel de la Minerve
53. Hotel Albergo del Senato
83. Hotel Rinascimento
84. Hotel Campo de' Fiori
85. Casa Banzo
86. Residenza in Farnese
87. Hotel Teatro di Pompeo

PIAZZA NAVONA

B: 46, 62, 64, 70, 81, 87, 116, 492, 628

● SNAPSHOT ●

The *centro storico*—"historical center"—of Rome covers an area stretching as far east as the Colosseum, and as far west as the Castel Sant' Angelo, across the Tiber River. Included in the *centro storico* is the Piazza Navona area nestled within the bend of the Tiber. The actual Piazza Navona, built in the oblong shape of an ancient racetrack, was constructed on the ruins of a stadium built by Emperor Domitian.

Today, the arena is decidedly Baroque, with fountains and a church created by two of that period's greatest artists, Bernini and Borromini. In some ways the lifestyle of the Piazza Navona area, too, is Baroque: booths of kitschy tourist souvenirs co-exist with posh restaurants and hip bars. By day it's all business; after dark it becomes a nocturnal Cinderella, attracting princes and chimney sweeps with its charm.

Piazza Navona itself and the winding streets of the *centro storico* are magnificent. Wander the streets. You can't get lost—the area is small enough to maneuver easily with a map. You'll feel like an explorer or relic hunter. Narrow byways, spectacular fountains, ancient churches, boisterous denizens—the area surrounding Piazza Navona can leave you breathless.

PLACES TO SEE
Landmarks:

In the first century, athletic games were held in a large stadium in what is today's ★**PIAZZA NAVONA (1)**. The piazza is a marvel of Baroque art and architecture. People flock there to sit and enjoy the sights and sounds of Rome's most famous piazza. Three incredible fountains grace the long esplanade. The **Fountain of the Four Rivers (2)**, designed by the master sculptor Bernini, depicts rivers that represent four continents: the Nile (Africa), Ganges (Asia), Danube (Europe), and Plata (South America). The other two fountains, the *Fountain of the Moor* and *Neptune's Fountain*, are also fabulous. Along the western flank of Piazza Navona is the **Sant'Agnese in Agone (3)** *(06-68.19.21.34, www.sant agneseinagone.org; hours: Tu–Sa 9:30AM–12:30PM, 3:30PM–7PM, Su, holidays 9AM–1PM, 4PM–8PM)* church, notable not only because it was made by Bernini's rival Borromini, but also because of the gutsy 13-year-old martyr it's named after. Agnes, a 4th-century girl, refused to renounce Christianity or marry the Roman suitors who fell for her. Some say she was stripped and strung out on the site, but her hair grew miraculously and covered her nude body. She was ultimately beheaded. Ruins of Emperor Domitian's stadium can be seen below the church.

TOP PICK!

Like much of Rome, the area abounds with churches and sculptured buildings. Walking through the quarter will bring you face to face with statues, columns, capitals, friezes, portals—all the drama and flamboyance of Renaissance and Baroque Rome. Raphael's famous *Sybils* fresco is the high point of **Santa Maria della Pace (4)** *(Vicolo del Arco della Pace 5, 06-686.11.56; hours: M, W, Sa 9AM–12PM, cloisters daily 10AM–11PM, exhibitions Tu–Su 10AM–8PM)*. And its lovely Bramante cloister has a bookshop and bar.

In 1575 Filippo Neri built **Chiesa Nuova (5)** *(P.za della Chiesa Nuova, 06-687.52.89, www.vallicella.org; hours: winter 7:30AM–12PM, 4:30PM–7PM, summer 7:30AM–12PM, 4:30PM–7:30PM)*, teaching humility to the Roman noblemen among his followers by making them do the work. Above and on either side of the altar are three Rubens paintings. For more Roman wit, make a beeline for **Pasquino (6)** *(P.za di Pasquino)*, the "talking" statue. Named after a 15th-century cobbler who wasn't fond of how the papacy curbed freedom of speech, Pasquino wrote out his gripes satirizing the ruling classes, then stuck them on the statue. Soon it became the rage to speak your mind through statues.

The spectacularly ornate **Palazzo Madama (7)** *(Corso del Rinascimento, 06-6706.2177, www.senato.it; hours: 1st Sa of month 10AM–6PM, closed Aug)*, once a Medici family palace, houses the Senate, the upper house of the

Italian parliament. Three Caravaggios hang in **San Luigi dei Francesi (8)** *(P.za di San Luigi dei Francesi 20, 06-688.271, www.saintlouis-rome.net; hours: F–W 10AM–12:30PM, 3PM–7PM, Th 10AM–12:30PM)*; his painting of St. Matthew as an old man, tired and with dirty feet, caused a stir in 16th-century Rome, where such a realistic portrayal of a saint was shocking.

Arts & Entertainment:

The **Museum of Rome (9)** *(Palazzo Braschi, P.za San Pantaleo 10, info and reservations 06-06.08, en.museo diroma.it; hours: Tu–Su 10AM–8PM)* gives glimpses of pre-modern Rome, covering the city's history from the Middle Ages to the 20th century. The ★**NATIONAL MUSEUM OF ROME—PALAZZO ALTEMPS (10)** *(P.za Sant'Apollinare 48, 06-39.96.77.00, www.roma2000.it/zmunaro.html; hours: Tu–Su 9AM–7:45PM)* holds part of the extraordinary state-owned collection of Roman stat-

TOP PICK!

ues and other artworks. The building went through a number of owners since construction began on it in the 15th century. Cardinal Marco Sittico Altemps acquired the palazzo in 1568. The Altemps lined their courtyard with ancient statues—which now are a core part of the museum's collection. This is the best place to view classical sculpture, and among the classics not to be missed are: *Arcs Ludovisi* (a warrior or god seated with a small cupid at his feet), *Galata's Suicide* (thought to have been commissioned by Julius Caesar to celebrate his triumph over the Gauls), and the *Ludovisi Throne* (with panels depicting the birth of Aphrodite and other Aphrodite scenes).

When cuts in funding threatened the respected **Teatro Valle (11)** *(Via del Teatro Valle 21, box office 06-689.6634, www.teatrovalleoccupato.it)* theatre with privatization, putting into question its artistic programming, the Occupy culture movement took over and workers in the arts and culture created Teatro Valle Occupato. Once host to Italian and international theater companies, the theatre is now a focal point for plays, performances, film screenings, festivals, and discussions on cultural politics and policy. The venue is as bewitching for its décor as its intellectual and cultural output. Founded in 1727, it was re-designed by Giuseppe Valadier, the 19th-century architectural superstar, and has remained fashionable to this day.

PLACES TO EAT & DRINK
Where to Eat:

Chef Gualtiero Marchesi's culinary artwork at **Hostaria dell'Orso (12)** (€€-€€€) *(Via dei Soldati 25C, 06-68.30.11.92, www.hdo.it; hours: M–Sa 8PM–1AM, bar: M–Sa 9PM–3AM, disco: Tu–Sa 11PM–4AM)* is matched by the elegant ambience of the 15th-century palazzo that was once an inn for pilgrims. Celeb chef Bartolomeo Cuomo reworks Roman favorites in his art-filled restaurant **Santa Lucia (13)** (€€-€€€) *(Largo Febo 12, 06-68.80.24.27, www.santaluciaristorante.it; hours: daily 12PM–3PM, 7PM–11PM, closed Jan)*.

Sleek and post-modern, **Antica Biblioteca (14)** (€€-€€€) *(Largo del Teatro Valle 9, 06-68.13.68.30, www.anticabibliotecavalle.com; hours: daily 8AM–11:30AM, 12PM–3PM, 8PM–11:30PM)* is definitely a product of globalization, with imaginative gastronomy. **Da Baffetto (15)** (€) *(Via del Governo Vecchio 114, 06-686.16.17, www.pizzeriabaffetto.it; hours: M 6PM–12AM, W 12PM–2:30PM, 6PM–12:30AM, Th–F 6PM–12:30AM, Sa–Su 12:30PM–3:30PM, 6:30PM–12:30AM)* is famous for its thin-crust pizzas and frenetic waiters.

Bars & Nightlife:

A sunset *aperitivo* at the rooftop bar of the hotel **Raphaël (16)** *(Largo Febo 2, 06-682.831, www.raphaelhotel.com; call for hours)* is pure magic: the light makes the buildings seem even pinker than they already are.

At **Bloom (17)** *(Via del Teatro Pace 30, 06-68.80.20.29; hours: M–Tu, Th–Sa 7PM–3AM, closed Jul & Aug)* very hip, very beautiful people mob the cocktail bar (an intense, sculpted affair in aluminum); DJs rock the 1940s interior after 12:30 AM. (Bloom is also a sushi bar—€€.) Nearby **Via della Pace (18)** is a trendy area full of bars and clubs. **Bar della Pace (19)** *(Via della Pace 3-4-5-7, 06-686.12.16, www.caffefellapace.it; hours: daily 9AM–2AM)* is fabulous, with a view to die for and a clientele of artists and film people. **La Maison (20)** *(Vicolo dei Granari 3, 06-683.33.12, www.lamaison-roma.com; call for hours)*, one of the hottest nightspots in Rome, has a different focus each night of the week: Tuesdays, *fashionistas*; Thursdays, showbiz celebs; Fridays, disco; Saturdays, special events; Sundays, gay/lesbian. **Casa Bleve (21)** *(Via del Teatro Valle 48-49, 06-686.59.70, www.casableve.it; hours: Tu–Sa 12:30PM–3PM, 7:30PM–11PM)* is the superstar of wine bars; this 14th-century coach house with restored arches, the remains of a Roman wall, and high ceilings is a great setting for sipping Italian wines. It's also a good spot for light lunches and after-dinner drinks.

WHERE TO SHOP

It's a delight to stroll down **Via dei Coronari (22)** and browse the shops for antiques and Art Nouveau pieces. **Via del Governo Vecchio (23)**, once part of the itinerary of papal processions (Via Papalis) between the Lateran and the Vatican in the 15th century, now packs fashionable stores among the 15th- and 16th-century houses. For example, **Josephine de Huertas & Co. (24)** *(Via del Governo Vecchio 68, 06-687.65.86, www.josephinedehuertas.com)* offers an eclectic mix of clothes with sensual fabrics, textures, and lines. Sleek and minimalist, **Luna & l'Altra (25)** *(P.za Pasquino 76, 06-68.80.49.95; hours: M 3:30PM–7:30PM, Tu–Sa 10AM–2PM, 3:30PM–7:30PM)* carries cutting edge designer fashions, from Dries Van Noten, Issey Miyake, and Martin Margiela to Limi feu, Zucca, Final Home, and Haat. The chicness of the clothes and accessories assures high hipness factor among the clientele. Look for vintage clothes at **Vestiti Usati Cinzia (26)** *(Via del Governo Vecchio 45, 06-683.29.45; hours: M–Sa 10AM–8PM, Su 2PM–8PM)*.

38

WHERE TO STAY

The atmosphere is classic, yet intimate, at **Hotel Due Torri (27)** (€-€€) *(Vicolo del Leonetto 23, 06-68.80.69.56, www.hotelduetorriroma.com)*, once home to cardinals and bishops. Simple, comfortable, and reasonably priced, **Hotel Portoghesi (28)** (€€) *(Via dei Portoghesi 1, 06-686.42.31, www.hotelportoghesiroma.it)* is situated in a 17th-century house. Weather permitting, breakfast is served on the rooftop terrace.

A regal 19th-century palazzo befitting its ornate décor, **Residenza Zanardelli (29)** (€-€€) *(Via G. Zanardelli 7, 06-68.21.13.92, www.hotelnavona.com)* is owned by a Roman aristocrat. This friendly architect enjoys making renovations that enhance the historical context of his building, including silk wallpaper and Versace tiles. The proprietor's other establishment, **Hotel Navona (30)** (€-€€) *(Via dei Sediari 8, 06-6830.1252, www.hotelnavona.com)*, is built on the ancient Baths of Agrippa. Antique ceilings, Baroque plasterwork, and Murano lamps add ambience.

Elegant, highly popular, and very expensive, the **Raphaël (31)** (€€€-€€€€) *(Largo Febo 2, 06-682.831, www.raphaelhotel.com)* is quiet, beautiful, and offers up-to-date facilities, such as a sauna, fitness center, and Internet access. Its two-level terrace, with bar and restaurant, is to-die-for romantic and has a magical view of the city, especially at sunset.

PANTHEON

B: 30, 40, 46, 62, 63, 64, 70, 81, 85, 87, 95, 116, 117, 119, 160, 175, 492, 628, 630, 850, 916

● SNAPSHOT ●

The Pantheon area is the financial district of Rome as well as the locale of many government buildings. Nearby you'll find the Palazzo Montecitorio (which houses the Italian parliament) and the stock exchange. In inimitable Italian style, serious businessmen and perfectly coiffed *contessas* mingle convivially with tourists, punks, and hippies. In fact, people-watching is one of the area's most popular sports, and two of the city's best known and most popular cafés are located in the Pantheon area: Tazza d'Oro and Caffè Sant'Eustachio. There are few things more delightful than claiming one of their outdoor tables and sitting in the reflected warmth of terra cotta and ivory-hued buildings while the descendants of an ancient people go about their cheerfully chaotic day.

PLACES TO SEE
Landmarks:

Layers upon layers, the ancient, medieval, Renaissance, and Baroque eras are all visible in the *centro storico*.

One of the oldest and most stunning buildings is the **★PANTHEON (32)** *(P.za della Rotonda, 06-68.30.02.30; hours: M–Sa 8:30AM–7:30PM, Su 9AM–6PM, holidays 9AM–1PM)*, first built by Marcus Agrippa in 27 BC, then rebuilt by Emperor Hadrian in AD 125. A temple to the gods of the Greco-Roman pan-

theon, it is a marvel of classical architecture and, along with the Colosseum, is one of the few ancient structures still intact. In 608 the **Pantheon (32)** was converted to a Christian church, which aided in its preservation. Outside it's imposing, but inside, the **Pantheon (32)** is glorious. Its breathtaking dome is a feat of 2nd-century engineering. Its height is exactly equal to its diameter, and there are no visible supporting structures. The only light in the **Pantheon (32)** comes through an opening at the apex of the dome. The building also houses the tombs of Victor Emmanuel II and Raphael.

Kitty-corner from the Pantheon is Rome's only Gothic church, **Santa Maria sopra Minerva (33)** *(P.za della Minerva 42, 06-679.39.26, www.basilicaminerva.it; hours: daily 8AM–7PM)*, built on the ruins of a temple of Minerva. Richly decorated, the church is a cornucopia of 15th- and 16th-century works of art, including Michelangelo's sculpture, *Christ the Redeemer*. The church is also the final resting place for several famous people, among them St. Catherine of Siena, Fra Angelico, and two 16th-century Medici popes. **Bernini's lovely elephant sculpture**, incongru-

41

ously burdened by an Egyptian obelisk on its back, stands in the piazza in front of the church.

The **Gesù (34)** *(P.za del Gesù, 06-69.70.01, www.chiesadelgesu.org; hours: daily 7AM–12:30PM, 4PM–7:45PM)* is the mother church of the Society of Jesus, or Jesuits; it was planned by the order's founder, Ignatius of Loyola, in 1551. Fierce anti-Protestantism is reflected in much of the lavish interior artwork and the Baroque architecture is typical of the Counter-Reformation period. The colonnade and remains of the **Temple of Hadrian (35)** *(La Borsa, P.za di Pietra, closed to public)*, built in AD 145 by his son, are incorporated in a 17th-century building, today's stock exchange. The **Piazza di Pietra**, in front of the temple ruins, is an especially magical spot in Rome; early in the morning, the sun crests over the rooftops, bathing the pink and yellow palazzi in warm light and illuminating the darkness behind Emperor Hadrian's columns. A block north, the **Column of Marcus Aurelius (36)** *(P.za Colonna)* is a second-century monument to the emperor's victories. Don't miss the wonderful **Galleria Alberto Sordi (37)** *(P.za Colonna 31-35, 06-69.19.07.69, www.galleriaalbertosordi.it; hours: M–Th 8:30AM–9PM, F–Sa 8:30AM–10PM, Su 9:30AM–9PM)*, a recently restored Art Deco arcade. The fabulous stucco ceiling decorations rival the beauty of the mosaic floors.

Arts & Entertainment:

Titian, Raphael, Caravaggio, Bruegel the Elder, and many other masters are represented in the collection of one of Rome's great aristocratic houses at **Palazzo Doria Pamphilj (38)** *(P.za del Collegio Romano 2, entrance Via* *del Corso 305, 06.679.73.23, www.doriapamphilj.it; hours: daily 9AM–7PM).* One of the star attractions here is the portrait of Pope Innocent X Pamphilj by Velázquez.

PLACES TO EAT & DRINK
Where to Eat:

Frenetic and fashionable, **Maccheroni (39) (€-€€)** *(P.za delle Coppelle 44, 06-68.30.78.95, www.ristorante maccheroni.com; hours: daily 1PM–3PM, 7:30PM–11:30PM)* is packed with politicians and beautiful people. The figs and ham, or Rome's signature dish, *pasta all'amatriciana*, are pretty fab too. The elegant **Osteria dell'Ingegno (40) (€€)** *(P.za di Pietra 45, 06-678.06.62; hours: M–Sa 12PM–3PM, 7PM–12AM)* offers inventive dishes, such as sweet and sour duck and fish couscous.

The décor at **La Rosetta (43) (€€€-€€€€)** *(Via della Rosetta 8, 06-686.1002, 06-68.30.88.41, www.larosetta. com; hours: M–Sa 12:45PM–2:45PM, 7:30PM–11PM, Su 7:30PM–11PM)* is elegant and simple; the food makes you forget everything else. From traditional to innovative, the fresh seafood never disappoints. The presentation is a work of art, and once you taste a mouthful, you'll never forget it.

Bars & Nightlife:
A trip to Rome isn't complete without going to the city's two best cafés. **Caffè Sant'Eustachio (41) (€)** *(P.za Sant'Eustachio 82, 06-68.80.20.48, www.santeustachioilcaffe.it; hours: Su–Th 8:30AM–1AM, F 8:30AM–1:30AM, Sa 8:30AM–2AM)* is famous for its coffee, made from a secret mix of coffee beans roasted on the premises. The specialty at **Tazza d'Oro (42) (€)** *(Via degli Orfani 84, 06-678.97.92, www.tazzadorocoffeeshop.com; call for hours)* is the *espresso granita*, thick iced coffee layered with whipped cream. Students might prefer **Habana Café (44)** *(Via dei Pastini 120, 06-678.19.83, habanaroma.com; hours: Tu–Su 11PM–4AM)*, with its live music, DJ sets, and casual, unpretentious atmosphere.

WHERE TO SHOP

Hard to say what's most interesting at **Degli Effetti (45)** *(P.za Capranica 75, 79, 93, 06-679.02.02, www.deglieffetti.eu)*, the gorgeous designer togs or the interior by the famous architect Massimiliano Fuksas. The gallery **Magazzino d'Arte Moderna (46)** *(Via dei Prefetti 17, 06-687.59.51, www.magazzinoartemoderna.com; hours: Tu–Sa 11AM–8PM)* showcases work by emerging graphic artists, photographers, and sculptors. Italian-designed kitchen apparatuses are both traditional and eclectic at **Art'è (47)** *(P.za Rondanini 32, 06-683.39.07; hours: M 1PM–7:30PM, Tu–Sa 9:30AM–7:30PM)*. Chocolatier to the Savoia kings, **Confetteria Moriondo e Gariglio (48)** *(Via di Piè di Marmo 21-22, 06-699.08.56; hours: daily 9AM–7:30PM)* has been making delectable truffles, marrons glacés, and other confections on the premises since 1886.

WHERE TO STAY

Charming, well furnished, and very comfortable, **Relais al Senato (49)** (€-€€) *(P.za Navona, Corsia Agonale 10, 06-68.80.98.59, 06-321.17.83, www.alsenato.it)* is a friendly B&B with modern conveniences. Refined and quiet, **Albergo Santa Chiara (50)** (€€-€€€) *(Via di Santa Chiara 21, 06-687.29.79, www.albergosantachiara.com)* offers good service and comfortable rooms. **Sole al Pantheon (51)** (€€-€€€) *(P.za della Rotonda 63, 06-678.04.41, www.hotelsolealpantheon.com)*, in a 15th-century palazzo, boasts ceilings with antique rafters and airy rooms. The opulent design of **Grand Hotel de la Minerve (52)** (€€€-€€€€) *(P.za della Minerva 69, 06-695.201, www.grandhoteldelaminerve.com)* includes a stained-glass ceiling in the lounge and large rooms with views of the church on the piazza and Bernini's elephant. Right in front of the Pantheon, in the midst of the *centro storico's* café life, is the small, lovely **Hotel Albergo del Senato (53)** (€€-€€€) *(P.za della Rotonda 73, 06-678.43.43, www.albergodelsenato.it)*. A bright breakfast room, rooftop terrace, and tasteful interiors add to the magic of its setting.

> Methinks I will not die quite happy without having seen something of that Rome of which I have read so much.
>
> —*Sir Walter Scott*

CAMPO DEI FIORI/GHETTO

B: 30, 40, 62, 63, 64, 70, 81, 87, 116, 271, 492, 628, 630, 780, 916

• SNAPSHOT •

Campo dei Fiori—"Field of Flowers"—was once the city's execution grounds. Now, it brims with life, especially in the mornings when farmers come to peddle fruits and vegetables in the open-air market. Narrow cobblestoned streets and colorful façades lend gaiety to the area, and streets are named after the tradesmen who once plied their crafts there. Via dei Cappellari, for example, means "Hatmakers' Street," Via dei Baullari, "Trunkmakers' Street," and Via dei Chiavari, "Lockmakers' Street." These roads give way to the imposing Palazzo Farnese and chic antique shops of Via Giulia by the river.

Along the river in the southeastern corner of the area is the **Ghetto**, where quaint narrow streets wind around ancient ruins. For over 2,000 years this picturesque neighborhood has been the locus of the oldest Jewish community in Europe. In the Middle Ages, the Catholic Church instated payment for protection, establishing a pattern of blackmail that brought times of both security and oppression to the community. Segregation even took the form of physical walls containing the Ghetto—facilitating protection and prejudice at the same time—as well as anti-Semitic laws. Today the Ghetto is known for its gastronomic delicacies as well as its extraordinarily beautiful sights, such as the *Fountain of the Tortoises* and the *Portico d'Ottavia*.

PLACES TO SEE
Landmarks:
Campo dei Fiori (54) *(P.za Campo dei Fiori)*—"Field of Flowers"—is the focal point of a vibrant neighborhood dominated by a colorful fruit and vegetable market. The square's history was just as colorful, attesting to papal power and abuse. In 1600, philosopher Giordano Bruno was burned at the stake here for heresy; a monument in his memory stands in the piazza today.

In contrast to Campo dei Fiori, the **Palazzo Farnese (55)** *(P.za Farnese, closed to public)* sets a dignified, austere tone. Much of it designed by Michelangelo, the majestic palace was built for Cardinal Alessandro Farnese, who became Pope Paul III. It has housed the French Embassy for well over a century. The other remarkable palace in the area, **Palazzo Spada (56)** *(P.za Capo di Ferro 13, 06-683.24.09, www.galleriaborghese.it; hours: Tu–Su 8:30AM–7:30PM)*, is like day to Farnese's night. Playful inside and out, Palazzo Spada's façade is covered in relief sculptures while an interior *trompe-l'oeil* (an optical illusion), by Borromini, makes a colonnaded gallery seem four times longer than it actually is. Today the palazzo is the grounds of the Italian State Council, but the **Galleria Spada (57)** *(see page 50)* museum is open to the public. More dramatic is **Sant'Andrea della Valle (58)** *(P.za Sant'Andrea della Valle, 06-686.13.39, www.sant-andrea-roma.it; hours: daily 7:30AM–12:30PM, 4:30PM–7:30PM)*, sufficiently flamboyant for Puccini to have made it the setting of the first act of *Tosca*.

Follow Corso Vittorio Emanuele II eastward to Largo Torre Argentina, where you'll find the **Largo Argentina Sacred Precincts (59)** *(Via San Nicola de' Cesarini)*, the ruins of four ancient temples which are some of the oldest in Rome. The **Crypta Balbi (60)** *(Via delle Botteghe Oscure 31, 06-3996.7700, archeoroma.beniculturali.it/en/museums; hours: Tu–Su 9AM–7:45PM)*, or Balbus's Crypt, part of the National Museum of Rome, is a stunning underground archaeological site which includes a lobby and a portico; an adjoining theater is still not excavated.

A few streets south you'll come to the delightful *Fontana delle Tartarughe*, the **Fountain of the Tortoises (61)** *(Piazza Mattei)*. Four bronze boys seem to be splashing in the fountain; each resting a foot on the head of a dolphin, they're triumphantly holding turtles up high in the air (the turtles were added nearly a century later). Equally impressive is the beautiful **Palazzo Mattei** *(entrances on Via dei Funari 31 or Via Caetani 32)* on the piazza. **Via Giulia (62)**, a long street that runs parallel to the river, is worth a lengthy walk. Full of palazzi built by the aristocracy, beautiful churches, and interesting shops, **Via Giulia (62)** was originally planned by Bramante, who designed St. Peter's Basilica.

The ancient ruins of the **Portico d'Ottavia (63)** *(Via Portico d'Ottavia)* were once the entrance to a large square with libraries and temples, built in honor of Octavia, sister of Emperor Augustus. All that remains are columns and a marble capping. Follow the walkway past three enormous columns—vestiges of the Temple of Apollo from the 5th century BC—until you come to the stunning, surreal **Theatre of Marcellus (64)** *(Via Teatro di Marcello)*. Originally an amphitheater commissioned by Julius Caesar and finished by Emperor Augustus, it had three tiers in Ionic, Doric, and Corinthian styles.

West of these ruins and through the Via del Portico d'Ottavia is the area known as the **Ghetto**, where a Jewish community settled in the 2nd century BC. The narrow streets have been witness to both prosperity and systematic persecution. The beautiful **Synagogue (65)** *(Lungotevere dei Cenci, 06-68.40.06.61; hours: mid-June–mid-Sept Su–Th 10AM–7PM, F 10AM–4PM, mid-Sept–mid-June Su–Th 10AM–5PM, F 9AM–2PM)* also contains the **Museum of Jewish Culture (66)** *(see page 50)*. From the **Ponte Fabricio** *(at Lungotevere dei Cenci, off of Via Portico d'Ottavia)*, the oldest functioning bridge, you can cross the Tiber to the island **Isola Tiberina (67)**, a peaceful refuge from the bustle and chaos across the river. The myth connected with the island says that in the 3rd century BC, Aesculapius, god of medicine, sailed down the Tiber to treat the plague. When his snake jumped out of the ship and onto the island, he knew that was where he had to set up a clinic. The church of San Bartolomeo on the main square was built on the ruins of the Temple of Aesculapius. A major hospital is located on the north side of the island, hopefully imbued with healing powers from the aura of its ancient mentor. By the southern tip is the **Ponte Rotto (68)** ("broken bridge"), the site of Rome's first stone bridge—*Pons Aemilius*, built in 142 BC. To the east, a tunnel on the shore is the entrance of **Cloaca Maxima** *(south of Ponte Palatino)*, the city sewer built by Etruscan kings in the 6th century BC and remodeled five centuries later.

Arts & Entertainment:

The delightful **Galleria Spada (57)** *(P.za Capo di Ferro 13, 06-683.24.09, www.galleriaborghese.it; hours: Tu–Su 8:30AM–7:30PM)* houses the collection of Cardinal Bernardino Spada and Virginio Spada, two brothers who amassed works by artists such as Rubens, Dürer, Orazio Gentileschi, Guercino, and Andrea del Sarto. **Piccola Farnesina (69)** *(Corso Vittorio Emanuele II 166A, 06-06.08, 06-68.80.68.48, www.museobarracco.it; hours: Oct–May Tu–Su 10AM–4PM, Jun–Sep Tu–Su 1PM–7PM)*, a lovely small palazzo, contains the Barracco Museum of Greek, Etruscan, and Egyptian sculpture, as well as Assyrian artifacts. The **Museum of Jewish Culture (66)** *(Lungotevere dei Cenci, 06-68.40.06.61, www.museo ebraico.roma.it; hours: mid-June–mid-Sept Su–Th*

10AM–7PM, F 10AM–4PM, mid-Sept–mid-June Su–Th 10AM–5PM, F 9AM–2PM) traces the history of the millennia-old Jewish community in Rome. Many well-known operas debuted at **Teatro Argentina (70)** (*Largo di Torre Argentina 52, 06-684.00.03.11/14, www.teatrodiroma.net*), none with as much drama as Rossini's *Barber of Seville*. When the audience booed the opera, Rossini insulted them; they retaliated by chasing him through the city.

PLACES TO EAT & DRINK
Where to Eat:
Romantic **Taverna Giulia (71)** (€€-€€€) (*Vicolo dell'Oro 23, 06-686.97.68, www.tavernagiulia.it; hours: M–Sa 12:30PM–3PM, 6:30PM–11PM, closed Aug*) specializes in exceptional Ligurian cuisine. You'd have to jump in the sea to get fish fresher than those served at **Assunta Madre (72)** (€€€-€€€€) (*Via Giulia 14, 06-68.80.69.72, www.assuntamadre.com; hours: M lunch, Tu–Su lunch & dinner*). It's a popular spot, with a delicious menu of unusual raw and cooked fish and seafood, and an unassuming, lovely, log cabin-like décor. The pleasant garden is open year-round, covered and heated in winter. The cheese selection at **Al Bric (73)** (€€-€€€) (*Via del Pellegrino 51, 06-687.95.33, www.albric.it; hours: Tu–Su 7:30PM–12AM*) is phenomenal. For a simple sandwich and a great coffee, try **Bar Farnese (74)** (€) (*Via dei Baullari 106, P.za Farnese, 06-68.80.21.25; call for hours*). It provides picturesque views of the Renaissance Palazzo Farnese and Roman humanity on its daily rounds.

The **Ghetto** is known for its many great restaurants. Informal and welcoming, **Al Pompiere (75)** (€€-€€€) *(Via Santa Maria dei Calderari 38, 06-686.83.77, www.alpompiereroma.com; call for hours, closed Su & Aug)* serves great authentic dishes, including the traditional salt cod *(baccalà)* with arugula *(rucola)*. Enjoy a Jewish riff on Roman cuisine at **Piperno (76)** (€€€-€€€€) *(Monte de Cenci 9, 06-68.80.66.29, www.ristorantepiperno.it; hours: Tu–Sa 12:45PM–2:20PM, 7:45PM–10:20PM, Su 12:45PM–2:20PM)*; the results include mouth-watering dishes with lots of garlic and olive oil.

Bars & Nightlife:

See and be seen at **La Vineria (77)** *(Campo dei Fiori 15, 06-68.80.32.68; hours: M–Sa 8:30AM–2AM)*, one of Rome's top spots for people-watching; it's best at cocktail hour.

WHERE TO SHOP

Many streets in Rome are known for certain types of wares. **Via del Pellegrino (78)** is lined with fabulous bookshops and art sellers. Along **Via dei Cappellari (79)**, furniture restorers work right out on the street. Stunning spectacles (eyeglasses and sunglasses) in brilliant colors are synonymous with **Mondello Ottica (80)** *(Via del Pellegrino 97-98, 06-686.19.55, www.mondelloottica.it; hours: M–Sa 9AM–1PM, 3:30PM–7:30PM)*. For great shoes at great prices, Roman women go to **Borini (81)** *(Via dei Pettinari 86-87, 06-687.56.70; hours: M 3:30PM–7:30PM, Tu–Sa 9:30AM–1PM, 3:30PM– 7:30PM)*. At the second-hand bookshop **Il museo del Louvre (82)** *(Via della Reginella 28, 06-68.80.77.25, www.ilmuseodellouvre.com; hours: M–Sa 11AM–2PM, 3:30PM–7:30PM)*, you'll find rare books, magazines, photographs, and 20th-century literature; there's also a gallery of photography, drawings, and prints. Home decorations at **Ilaria Miani (88)** *(Via Monserrato 35, 06-683.31.60, www.ilariamiani.it)* include paintings, lamps, lampshades, and various interesting decorative pieces.

WHERE TO STAY

The rooms at friendly **Hotel Rinascimento (83)** (€-€€€) *(Via del Pellegrino 122, 06-68.80.95.56, www.hotel rinascimento.com)* are small, but, depending on the season, can be a good deal. You'll love the views from the rooftop terrace of **Hotel Campo de' Fiori (84)** (€€-€€€) *(Via del Biscione 6, 06-68.80.68.65, www.hotelcampodefiori.com)*; the décor is ornately appointed with antique touches. **Casa Banzo (85)** (€) *(Via Monte di Pietà 30, 06-683.3909, www.casabanzo.it)*, a B&B housed in a beautiful 15th-century palazzo with a lovely courtyard, is quiet, elegant, and full of antiques. Spacious, well-furnished rooms and a lovely rooftop terrace are what you can expect at **Residenza in Farnese (86)** (€-€€) *(Via del Mascherone 59, 06-68.21.09.80, www.residenzafarnese roma.it)*. The hotel is centrally located, quiet, comfortable, and friendly; the cornucopia of fresh fruit and breakfast foods makes a good start to the day. On the remains of the Theater of Pompey, where Caesar was assassinated in 44 BC, **Hotel Teatro di Pompeo (87)** (€€) *(Largo del Pallaro 8, 06-687:28.12/06-68.30.01.70, www.hotelteatrodipompeo.it)* offers small but pleasing rooms with unpretentious décor.

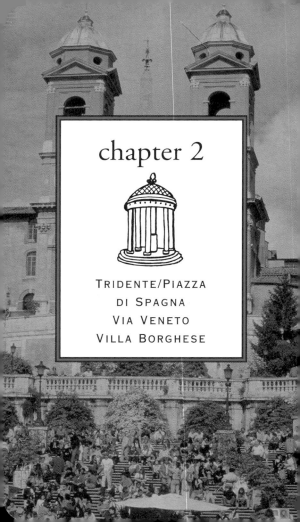

chapter 2

TRIDENTE/PIAZZA
DI SPAGNA
VIA VENETO
VILLA BORGHESE

TRIDENTE/PIAZZA DI SPAGNA VIA VENETO VILLA BORGHESE

Places to See:
1. Porta del Popolo
2. Piazza del Popolo
3. Santa Maria del Popolo
4. Ara Pacis
5. Mausoleum of Augustus
9. SPANISH STEPS ★
10. Boat Fountain
11. Pincio Gardens
12. Keats-Shelley Memorial House
13. Casa-Museo Giorgio De Chirico
30. Santa Maria della Vittoria
31. Piazza Barberini
32. Santa Maria della Concezione
33. Palazzo Barberini/Piazza di Spagna
48. Temple of Diana
49. Temple of Aesculapius
50. Bioparco
51. GALLERIA BORGHESE ★
52. National Gallery of Modern Art
53. Villa Giulia

Places to Eat & Drink:
14. Dal Bolognese
15. Gina
16. Rhome
17. Bar Canova
18. Caffè Greco
19. Gregory's
34. La Terrazza dell'Eden
35. Papà Baccus
36. Ristorante Césarina
37. Moma
38. Jasmine
39. Suggestum
40. Café de Paris
41. Doney
42. San Marco
54. Oliver Glowig
55. Art Cafè

Where to Shop:
6. Via dei Condotti
7. Via Borgognona
8. Via Frattina
20. Battistoni
21. Via Bocca di Leone
22. Sermoneta
23. Il Discount dell'Alta Moda

★ *Top Picks*

24. Piazza di San Lorenzo in Lucina
43. Albertina
44. Brioni
45. Aston
46. Michel Harem
56. Galleria Borghese Museum Shop

Where to Stay:
25. Hotel de Russie
26. Il Palazzetto
27. Hotel Scalinata di Spagna
28. Hotel Hassler
29. Hotel Marcus 939 Rome
47. Aleph Hotel

All roads lead to Rome.

—Proverb

TRIDENTE/PIAZZA DI SPAGNA

B: 116, 117, 119
M: A to Spagna

• SNAPSHOT •

The Tridente, an area extending southward from the Piazza del Popolo and including the Piazza di Spagna on the eastern border, gets its name from the three boulevards forking downward from Piazza del Popolo. The streets Via del Babuino, Via del Corso, and Via di Ripetta form a trident encompassing Rome's most posh area. Along with Via Veneto, the Tridente celebrates the glitz and glamour of the "jet set" immortalized in Federico Fellini's 1960 classic film *La Dolce Vita*. Aesthetes and artists have flocked to this quarter, along with film directors, actors, and international designers. For decades, it was a magnet for international literati, such as Keats, Shelley, and Byron.

Today, the Tridente is the most luxurious area of Rome, a mecca for high-style shoppers that is distinguished by its international ambience. Many of the city's most dignified hotels and distinctive restaurants are located in this quarter. Don't miss the Spanish Steps, rising above the Piazza di Spagna. From there, the gloriously breathtaking vista reminds you why Rome is the Eternal City.

PLACES TO SEE
Landmarks:

In the 3rd century the **Aurelian Wall** was constructed to protect the city from invaders, with entrance and exit portals at various points. The 16th-century **Porta del Popolo (1)** gateway was built by Pope Pius IV (Medici) on the site of the ancient *Porta Flaminia* as an impressive first view of Rome for VIP visitors entering from the north. Just inside the Porta del Popolo is the grandiose square **Piazza del Popolo (2)**. For centuries it was the papacy's preferred execution grounds. The square, one of Rome's largest, is lavish in architecture and artistry. Twin churches on the southern end of the enormous oval are remarkable in their neoclassical beauty. In the center, an ancient Egyptian obelisk is flanked by fountains with enormous marble lions spouting water from their mouths.

The church **Santa Maria del Popolo (3)** *(P.za del Popolo 12, 06-361.08.36, www.santamariadelpopolo.it; hours: M–Sa 7AM–12PM, 4PM–7PM, Su 8AM–1:30PM, 4:30PM–7:15PM)* is one of Rome's gems of early Renaissance art, built in 1472 by Pope Sixtus IV della Rovere. It was said that Emperor Nero was secretly buried on the site; folk legend says that demons haunted the area, torturing Nero for his crimes, until the first church was built there in 1099. South of Piazza del Popolo, the **Ara Pacis (4)** *(Via di Ripetta/Lungotevere in Augusta, 06-06.08, www.arapacis.it; hours: Tu–Su 9AM–7PM)*, "Altar of Peace," is a monument and museum commemorating Emperor Augustus's conquest of Gaul and Spain and the ensuing peace. The area south of the monument was once the site of the **Mausoleum of Augustus (5)** *(P.za Augusto Imperatore; not open to the public)*, where the emperor's ashes were buried.

If ancient memorials aren't your cup of tea, you can join the thousands who gladly pay homage—and empty their wallets—to modern emperors of fashion and design in the well-planned streets between **Via del Corso** and **Via del Babuino**. **Via dei Condotti (6)**, "Street of the Conduits," named after the ducts that brought water to the Baths of Agrippa near the Pantheon, is the most famous of these, closely followed by **Via Borgognona (7)** and **Via Frattina (8)**.

TOP PICK!

One of the most popular spots in Rome is the ★**SPANISH STEPS (9)** *(Piazza di Spagna)*, named for the Spanish Embassy to the Vatican, housed near the base of the stairs. Built in grand Gallic style by a French financier between 1723 and 1726, they form an elegant staircase rising up the slope from **Piazza di Spagna (33)** to the church of **Trinità dei Monti** *(P.za Trinità dei Monti 3, 06-679.41.79; hours: daily 10AM–1PM, 4PM–6:30PM)* on Pincio Hill. In spring and summer, urns of azaleas are displayed on the steps, and fashion shows are held there. The area has been

59

beloved of writers, artists, and musicians since the 18th century, most notably Keats, Shelley, and De Chirico. At the foot of the Spanish Steps is the delightfully quirky **Boat Fountain (10)** *(P.za di Spagna)*, representing a leaky old boat that was said to have been stranded there when the Tiber overflowed.

From the top of the Steps, follow Viale della Trinità dei Monti to the **Pincio Gardens (11)** *(Pincio Hill)* for a fabulous view of Rome. Rock formations, magnificent tree-lined walks, and lovely benches make the elegant gardens, designed by 19th-century star architect Giuseppe Valadier, a favorite place for afternoon strolls or picnics.

Arts & Entertainment:

On Piazza di Spagna are two museum houses dedicated to artists who lived and worked there. The **Keats-Shelley Memorial House (12)** *(Piazza di Spagna 26, 06-678.42.35, www.keats-shelley-house.org; hours: M–Sa 10AM–1PM, 2PM–4PM)*, the dusty pink building at the bottom of the Spanish Steps, contains all sorts of memorabilia related to the two English poets. Keats died there in 1821 at the age of 25, succumbing to tuberculosis and depression over bad reviews of his poetry. Both Keats and Shelley are buried in Rome's Protestant Cemetery *(see page 152)*. More than 100 years later, another great artist died nearby, and his work space is now a museum: **Casa-Museo Giorgio De Chirico (13)** *(P.za di Spagna 31, 06-*

679.65.46, www.fondazionedechirico.org; hours: by appt. Tu–Sa & 1st Su of month 10AM–1PM, closed Aug) displays the palettes, brushes, and paints the Surrealist painter was working with just before his death, as well as other favorite objects and books.

PLACES TO EAT & DRINK
Where to Eat:

An excellent choice for traditional food, **Dal Bolognese (14) (€-€€)** *(P.za del Popolo 1-2, 06-361.14.26; hours: Tu–Su 1PM–3PM, 8:15PM–12AM; closed 3 wks in Aug)* claims that "all Rome" comes by at some time or another. The view of the piazza and Pincio Hill, opposite, is great too. Hike up Pincio or to Villa Borghese with a picnic basket from **Gina (15) (€)** *(Via San Sebastianello 7/A, 06-678.02.51, www.ginaroma.com; hours: daily 11AM–8PM)* or sit inside the cool white rooms and feel summery all year round. A modern, comfortable décor and innovative Italian cuisine create a blend of "Rome" and "home" at **Rhome (16) (€-€€)** *(P.za Augusto Imperatore 42-48, 06-68.30.14.30, www.rhomerestaurant.it; hours: Su–F 12PM–3PM, 8PM–11:30PM, Sa 8PM–11:30PM, book ahead)*, a hotspot where traditional dishes are given surprising twists.

Bars & Nightlife:

Piazza del Popolo was one of the spots where, up until the early 1990s, you could spot Italian movie stars and notables all the time. The back room at **Bar Canova (17)** *(P.za del Popolo 16-17, 06-361.22.31, www.canova piazzadelpopolo.it; hours: daily 8AM–12/1AM)* has been dedicated to Fellini, who lived nearby in Via Margutta 110 and regularly popped in for breakfast or an espresso.

The historic **Caffè Greco (18)** *(Via dei Condotti 86, 06-679.17.00, www.anticocaffegreco.eu; hours: daily 9AM–8PM, closed 10 days Aug)* was made famous by the artists and intellectuals who congregated there: Goethe, Byron, Keats, Liszt, Wagner, Bizet, Schopenhauer; then there were those, like Casanova and mad Bavarian King Ludwig, who also added color and notoriety to the place. **Gregory's (19)** *(Via Gregoriana 54A, 06-679.63.86, www.gregorysjazz.com; hours: Tu–Su 7PM–2AM)* is a cozy venue for good jazz and blues.

WHERE TO SHOP

High fashion is the name of the game in the Tridente. Haute couture pops from the windows of Renaissance palazzi in **Via dei Condotti (6)**, the street famous for designer shops, where you'll find Prada, Gucci, Ferragamo, Armani, and the most Roman of designers, Valentino. The gorgeous courtyard of **Battistoni (20)** *(Via dei Condotti 60-61a, 06-697.61.11, www.battistoni.com)* prepares you for the refinement inside. It's the epitome

of the elegant Italian shop for classic, distinguished custom-made men's tailoring (although they also tailor for women).

In the next street over, **Via Borgognona (7)**, the showrooms include Fendi, Moschino, Zegna, and Versace (men). For designers like Mariella Burani and Versace (women), it's **Via Bocca di Leone (21)**. Extraordinary handstitched gloves are the exemplary item at **Sermoneta (22)** *(P.za di Spagna 61, 06-679.19.60, www.sermonetagloves.com; hours: M–Sa 9:30AM–8PM, Su 10AM–7PM)*—not just cashmere, wool, and kid, but ostrich, boar, and crocodile, in sixty colors and six sizes.

If all the high-fashion boutiques leave you yearning for designer togs but your wallet keeps resisting, fear not: **Il Discount dell'Alta Moda (23)** *(Via di Gesù e Maria 14-16a, 06-322.50.06, 06-361.37.96; hours: M 2PM–7:30PM, Tu–Su 10:30AM–1:30PM, 2PM–7:30PM)* offers last season's designer clothes (men's and women's) at up to an 80% discount. For a sense of old-fashioned Roman life, head to **Piazza di San Lorenzo in Lucina (24)**: the shops are classic, and the street life is delightfully relaxed.

WHERE TO STAY

Originally designed by Giuseppe Valadier, the 19th-century architect who laid out the **Pincio Gardens (11)** *(see page 60)*, as a residence for the Russian czar, **Hotel de Russie (25)** (€€€€) *(Via del Babuino 9, 06-32.88.81, www.hotelderussie.it)* is among Europe's top luxury hotels—and very expensive. Elegant in a modern reincarnation of its classical past, it has attracted famous artists, such as Picasso and Stravinsky.

Simplicity as luxury defines the four rooms of the **Il Palazzetto (26)** (€€-€€€) *(Vicolo del Bottino 8, 06-699.34.10.00, www.ilpalazzettoroma.com)* just off Piazza di Spagna. The roof terrace has wonderful views and hosts lovely wine tastings. Reasonable for the area, **Hotel Scalinata di Spagna (27) (€€-€€€)** *(P.za Trinità dei Monti 17, 06-69.94.08.96, booking 06-679.30.06, www.hotelscalinata.com)* immerses you in a sense of luxury with its beautiful woodwork, exquisite gold-framed mirrors, and decidedly pampering chaise longues.

The exclusive **Hotel Hassler (28) (€€€€)** *(P.za Trinità dei Monti 6, 06-699.340, booking 06-69.93.47.55, www.hotelhasslerroma.com)* is steeped in prestige, refinement, and beauty. Paintings, silk tapestries, and wood paneling decorate the rooms with harmony and elegance, while dataports and other modern conveniences lend practicality. The rooftop restaurant is graced with magnificent views of Rome. The lovely, renovated **Hotel Marcus 939 Rome (29) (€-€€)** *(Via del Clementino 94, 06-68.30.03.12, www.hotel939.com)* offers a luxury feeling at an affordable price.

VIA VENETO

B: 52, 53, 63, 80, 95, 116, 119
M: A to Barberini

• SNAPSHOT •

The quarter gets its name from the street, Via Veneto, that snakes through what was once the Ludovisi family estate. In the 1870s, after Italian Unification, Villa Ludovisi went the way of many aristocratic palaces and gardens. It was sold off to speculators who built ostentatious *palazzi* in the area. By the 1950s and 1960s, the newly booming film industry gave an international patina to Via Veneto, and the quarter became the hot spot for celebrities. Cinecittà, Italy's Hollywood, welcomed U.S. productions in the 1950s, and their stars flocked to Via Veneto.

In 1960, Via Veneto was the central locale of Fellini's *La Dolce Vita*, a satire of the decadent lifestyles of the rich. The term *paparazzo* arose from the character of the same name in the film, a photographer who snapped pictures of the beautiful people. That same year, Luchino Visconti's *Rocco and His Brothers* and Michelangelo Antonioni's *L'Avventura* won awards. Rome is, of course, the centerpiece of Roberto Rossellini's *Rome, Open City*, his paean to the *Caput Mundi*. In more recent times, Cinecittà has seen a reawakening, with films like Nanni Moretti's *Caro Diario*, Roberto Benigni's *Life Is Beautiful*, Anthony Minghella's *The Talented Mr. Ripley*, Martin

Scorsese's *Gangs of New York*, and the blockbuster *Ocean's Twelve* shooting in studios or on location in the city.

PLACES TO SEE
Landmarks:

It's worth a visit to **Santa Maria della Vittoria (30)** *(Via XX Settembre 17, 06-42.74.05.71, www.chiesasmaria vittoria.191.it; hours: daily 7AM–12PM, 3:30PM–7PM)* just to see Bernini's sculpture *The Ecstasy of St. Teresa of Avila*. Italian artists have never shied away from putting rapture, religious or otherwise, on public display—and this St. Teresa is unquestionably in ecstasy. The 16th-century Spanish mystic is confronted by an angel with a golden spear—whether to protect or smite is not clear. Some say Teresa is experiencing divine joy; others claim it may be of a more somatic nature.

In **Piazza Barberini (31)**, ancients performed erotic Dionysian dances to welcome spring. Today Bernini's fabulous **Triton Fountain** makes up for the less than erotic atmosphere of traffic and exhaust fumes. The sea god Triton sits on a shell, his fish tail curled beneath him, and blows water through a conch. Don't miss the small **Fountain of the Bees**, a drinking fountain in a corner of the piazza. Bees were the Barberini family symbol.

Via Veneto winds its way gracefully from Piazza Barberini upward to **Porta Pinciana**, another arched gateway in the

Aurelian Wall and an entrance to the Villa Borghese. A walk along the street once made glamorous by international film stars takes you past posh over-priced sidewalk cafés, opulent hotels, and the **Palazzo Margherita** *(Via Vittorio Veneto 119/a, 06-46.741)*, once a Ludovisi palazzo, now the U.S. Embassy. An uncharacteristically Goth spot along the tourist-crowded street is **Santa Maria della Concezione (32)** *(Via Veneto 27, 06-45.28.50, Crypt 06-88.80.36.95, www.cappucciniviaveneto.it; hours: Church daily 7AM–12PM, 3PM–7PM, Crypt daily 9AM–7PM)*; in its underground crypt, the bones and skulls of thousands of Capuchin friars ornament the walls of several vaulted chapels.

Arts & Entertainment:

The **Palazzo Barberini (33)** *(Via delle Quattro Fontane 13, 06-482.41.84, www.galleriaborghese.it; hours: Tu–Su 8:30AM–7PM)*, built by Pope Urban VIII Barberini for his family in the early 17th century, houses the **Galleria Nazionale d'Arte Antica**, a significant museum. Works by Filippo Lippi, Caravaggio, and Hans Holbein the Younger are among many important pieces. *La Fornarina*, a famous painting believed to be of Raphael's mistress, is bold in its sensual coyness, with the mostly naked woman suggestively cupping her intimate parts with her hands.

PLACES TO EAT & DRINK
Where to Eat:

Dining around Via Veneto can be an expensive proposition but is often worth it. For a romantic candlelight dinner beneath the splendid cityscape, try **La Terrazza dell'Eden (34) (€€€€)** *(Via Ludovisi 49, 06-47.81.27.52,* *www.laterrazzadelleden.com, www.edenroma.com; hours: daily 12:30PM–2:30PM, 7:30PM–10:30PM).* **Papà Baccus (35) (€€-€€€)** *(Via Toscana 36, 06-42.74.28.08, www.papabaccus.com; call for hours, closed Sa lunch, & Su)* serves authentic dishes using products shipped in from Tuscany. The service makes you feel like you're their best guest. Marcello Mastroianni and Federico Fellini, among many other notables, have dined at mainstay **Ristorante Césarina (36) (€-€€)** *(Via Piemonte 109, 06-42.01.34.32 or 06-488.08.28, www.ristorante cesarinaroma.it, call for hours, closed Su)*, featuring Romagna specialties and stews.

Sleek, chic, and ultramodern, **Moma (37) (€€-€€€)** *(Via San Basilio 42-43, 06-42.01.17.98, www.ristorante moma.it; hours: M–Sa 12:30PM–3PM, 7:30PM–12AM)* does a revision of traditional Italian and foreign cuisines. For good, inexpensive Chinese food, **Jasmine (38) (€)** *(Via Sicilia 45, 06-42.88.49.83; call for hours)* is the answer.

Bars & Nightlife:

Café/bar **Suggestum (39)** *(Via Vittorio Veneto 14, 06-481.97.08; call for hours)* is a nice spot for coffee or a light meal. The upstairs tearoom of **Café de Paris (40)** *(Via Vittorio Veneto 90, 06-42.01.22.57, www.cafede parisroma.eu; hours: Su–Th 8AM–1AM, F–Sa 8AM–2AM)* is an icon of *la dolce vita*. The pastries are delectable, and there's a good selection of teas. Ava Gardner, Richard Burton, and Burt Lancaster (not together) were patrons of the bar **Doney (41)** *(Via Vittorio Veneto 141, 06-47.08.27.83, www.westinrome.com/en/doney; hours: daily 8AM–1AM)*. Claim a spot on one of the sidewalk sofas and watch the beautiful people go by. Andy Warhol quotations bedeck the walls at **San Marco (42)** *(Via Sardegna 38d, 06-42.82.48.93; call for hours)*, a wine bar with patio that doubles as restaurant/pizzeria/grill.

WHERE TO SHOP

Via Veneto is the place to go for conservative, refined clothing. Classic Italian knitwear seems to weather the decades; you might find the perfect piece at **Albertina (43)** *(Via Lazio 20, 06-488.58.76)*. Well-to-do gentlemen have been going to **Brioni (44)** *(Via Barberini 79-81, 06-48.45.17, www.brioni.com)* forever for the perfect three-piece suit. **Aston (45)** *(Via Boncompagni 27, 06-42.87.12.27, www.astontessuti.it)* carries designer fabrics, unique both in texture and print. Part flea market, part antique shop, **Michel Harem (46)** *(Via Sistina 137, 06-481.44.68)* carries eclectic curios and wacky *follie*.

WHERE TO STAY

Sensual and deliciously inviting, the **Aleph Hotel (47)** (€€-€€€) *(Via di San Basilio 15, 06-42.29.01, www.boscolo hotels.com)* plays a game between red and white-and-black color schemes. New York architect Adam Tihany designed the place to reflect the contradictions of Rome—purity and decadence, heaven and hell, divine and devilish. Rooms are blissful.

VILLA BORGHESE

B: 52, 53, 88, 95, 116, 490, 495

• SNAPSHOT •

Many of Rome's aristocratic families produced popes, who in turn gave further clout to the clans, often building majestic palaces on lands they already owned or soon bought. Camillo Borghese became Pope Paul V (1605–1621), ringing in an era of enormous power and profit for his family. Nephew Scipione, an aficionado of the arts who soon became a cardinal, built the Villa Borghese on the family's vineyards and bought much of the surrounding land. It was a dramatic statement and a model to which other prominent families looked when constructing their own estates: Villa Ludovisi, Villa Farnese, and Villa Doria Pamphilj, among others. Today, the state-owned Villa Borghese is a superb public park, replete with museums, gardens, lakes, arbors, fountains, neoclassical temples, statues, and a plethora of jogging paths and picnic grounds. Centrally located, it offers Romans and visitors alike a respite from city living, all within walking distance of the cheerful chaos. Rental bikes make it easier to cover the grounds *(for rentals, see page 14)*.

PLACES TO SEE
Landmarks:

The ★**VILLA BORGHESE** is the perfect place to recover if you've overdosed on culture and the city. It's great for jogging, boating, strolling, or picnicking. If you've not had your fill of art and history, it also contains great museums and a zoo. Along your walks, don't miss the **Temple of Diana (48)**, a round, open-air neoclassical structure between **Porta Pinciana** and Piazza di Siena. Many of the structures were made in the Baroque period to look like ancient temples. The **Temple of Aesculapius (49)**, in the artificial lake of the *Giardino del Lago*, is a neoclassical monument in Ionian style. The **Bioparco (50)** (*Viale del Giardino Zoologico, 06-360.82.11, www.bioparco.it; hours: daily 9:30AM–5/6PM*)—a zoo, conservation center, and zoological museum (with sections on biodiversity and habitats of the Lazio Province)—is in the northeast corner of the park.

TOP PICK!

Arts & Entertainment:

The hedonistic Cardinal Scipione Borghese, who concocted the villa and park, was a patron of the arts. His palazzo is now the ★**GALLERIA BORGHESE (51)** (*Piazzale Scipione Borghese 5, 06-841.39.79, box office 06-328.10, www.galleriaborghese.it; hours: Tu–Su 8:30AM–7:30PM*), which houses the spectacular

TOP PICK!

private Borghese collection. The ground floor is dedicated to sculpture, while paintings are displayed on the upper floor. Some of the highlights are Titian's *Sacred and Profane Love*, Bernini's *Apollo and Daphne*, and Canova's *Pauline Borghese* (Napoleon's sister, Prince Camillo Borghese's wife). When Camillo saw the nearly-naked marble *Pauline*, he locked up the statue, forbidding even Canova to see it once it was done. Caravaggio, in his painting *David with the Head of Goliath*, did a self-portrait as the decapitated Goliath; it revealed his terror at possibly being guillotined for murdering a tennis opponent. He was eventually pardoned for the crime.

The **National Gallery of Modern Art (52)** *(Viale delle Belle Arti 131, 06-32.29.81, www.gnam.beniculturali.it; hours: Tu–Su 8:30AM–7:30PM)*, housed in a beautiful neoclassical palazzo, is a collection of 19th- and 20th-century art. It includes Italian artists such as Canova, de Chirico, Morandi, and Modigliani, as well as foreign masters such as Cézanne, van Gogh, Rodin, and Klimt.

The **Villa Giulia (53)** *(Piazzale di Villa Giulia 9, 06-322.65.71/06-320.19.51/17.06, villagiulia.beniculturali.it; hours: Tu–Su 8:30AM–7:30PM)*, a museum covering pre-Roman epochs, is the most significant Etruscan museum in Italy. The Etruscans, an ancient civilization whose origins are unknown, ruled Rome in the 7th and 6th centuries BC. By the 1st century BC, they had been integrated into the Roman empire.

PLACES TO EAT & DRINK
Where to Eat:

It's worth a trek to the northern border of Villa Borghese to the exclusive Aldrovandi Palace Hotel, where one of Italy's newest star chefs opened his eponymous Roman restaurant **Oliver Glowig (54)** (€€€-€€€€) *(Via Ulisse Aldrovandi 15, 06-321.61.26, 06-322.39.93, www.oliverglowig.com, www.aldrovandi.com; hours: Tu–Sa 12:30PM–2:30PM, 7:30PM–10:30PM)*. Dining in the spectacular garden is an amazing experience. Glowig has earned two Michelin stars and his surprising, unique combination of flavors and textures is exciting and creative.

Bars & Nightlife:

Well into the morning hours, the **Art Cafè (55)** *(Viale del Galoppatoio 33, 06-36.00.65.78, www.art-cafe.it; hours: Tu–Su 7:30PM–3AM)* is a happening place. From June to August, it's hopping with live music, performances, art installations, and fashion shows. In winter the whole shebang simply moves into the Villa Borghese car park.

WHERE TO SHOP

While in the **Galleria Borghese (51)**, check out the **Galleria Borghese Museum Shop (56)** *(Piazzale del Museo Borghese 5, 06-855.73.77, www.galleriaborghese.it; hours: Tu–Su 8:30AM–7:30PM)*, which offers museum reproductions, jewelry, books, and a wide variety of gifts.

chapter 3

QUIRINALE/TREVI
ESQUILINO & MONTI
SAN LORENZO

Quirinale/Trevi
Esquilino & Monti
San Lorenzo

Places to See:

1. TREVI FOUNTAIN ★
2. Santa Maria in Trivio
3. Via della Pilotta
4. Palazzo del Quirinale
5. Piazza della Repubblica
6. Terme di Diocleziano
7. San Luca National Academy of Art
8. Pasta Museum
9. Palazzo Colonna
10. Museo Nazionale di Roma: Terme di Diocleziano
11. Santa Maria degli Angeli
12. Aula Ottagona
13. Teatro dell'Opera
14. Scuderie del Quirinale
15. Palazzo delle Esposizioni
27. SANTA MARIA MAGGIORE ★
28. SAN PIETRO IN VINCOLI ★
29. Domus Aurea
30. Parco del Colle Oppio
31. Galleria Termini/GATE
46. San Lorenzo fuori le Mura
47. Galleria Pino Casagrande

Places to Eat & Drink:

16. L'Antica Birreria Peroni
17. Trattoria Tritone
18. Il Gelato di San Crispino
19. Trimani
32. Agata e Romeo
33. F.I.S.H.
34. Hasekura
35. Al Vino Al Vino
36. Bohemien
37. Fiddler's Elbow
48. Vinosteria
49. Formula 1
50. Pommidoro
51. Tram Tram
52. Ferrazza

Where to Shop:

20. Feltrinelli International
21. Trimani
22. Il Giardino di Domenico Persiani
38. Panella
39. La Bottega del Cioccolato
40. Le Gallinelle
41. Termini Train Station
42. L'Artigianaio Orologi
53. Claudio Sano
54. Aspecifico Atelier Myriam B

★ *Top Picks*

Where to Stay:
23. Hotel Exedra
24. St. Regis Grand
25. Residenza Cellini
26. Flowerome
43. Radisson Blu es
44. Residenza Monti
45. Antica Locanda

QUIRINALE/TREVI

B: Quirinale—H, 40, 64, 70, 170, routes along Via del Nazionale; Trevi—52, 53, 61, 62, 63, 71, 80, 95, 116, routes along Via del Corso and Via del Tritone; Repubblica—36, 60, 61, 62, 64, 84, 90, 170, 175, 492, 649, 910

M: A to Repubblica

• SNAPSHOT •

Rome was built on seven hills: Quirinale, Viminale, Esquilino, Celio, Campidoglio or Capitolino, Palatino, and Aventino. Other city hills—the Gianicolo, Colle Oppio, and Velia—are not listed among the official seven. The Quirinale was residential during the Empire and the first to be rediscovered and developed during the Renaissance. Whoever had enough money to get away from the insalubrious low ground moved up to the hills. In the late 16th century, the papacy moved to the Palazzo Quirinale, its summer residence at the top of the hill, away from the smelly, malaria-infested Tiber. Aristocratic families, such as the Colonna and Aldobrandini, built palaces on the hill as well. Italian Unification in 1870 marked the end of papal rule. Rome was made the capital of the new nation, and the papacy vacated the Palazzo Quirinale, which became the royal palace and later the presidential palace.

PLACES TO SEE
Landmarks:

TOP PICK!

The overpowering ★**TREVI FOUNTAIN (1)** takes up most of the space of the small Piazza di Trevi. Atop large boulders, marble statues depict the sea god Neptune riding in a chariot pulled by two sea horses. Two tritons manage them, one sea horse unruly, the other calm—the two opposing aspects of the ocean. Salubrity and Abundance oversee the scene from the background. In niches above the fountain, along the back wall, are statues memorializing the history of the 15.5-mile-long conduit, the Acqua Vergine, that brought water to the Quirinale. One represents Rome, the terminus of the canal; the other, the virgin (for whom the aqueduct was named), who

showed the Roman soldiers the spring from which the water was drawn. The modern Trevi myth is that if you toss a coin into the fountain, you'll return to Rome—a practice immortalized in the 1954 film *Three Coins in the Fountain*. Once a week the basin is cleaned and the coins collected and donated to the Italian Red Cross.

Rome is full of playful, quirky spots. Around the corner from the Trevi Fountain, **Santa Maria in Trivio (2)** *(P.za dei Crociferi 49, 06-678.96.45; hours: daily 8AM or 10AM–12PM, 4PM–7PM)* looks like just a façade, as though it were glued onto the building behind it. It even has fake windows! One of the more delightful spots in Rome is just a few streets away, the **Via della Pilotta (3)**. Its succession of romantic arches takes you back to days when illicit lovers, caped and hooded, furtively ran through the arcades to secret assignations.

Wind your way via staircases and sloping streets up the hill to **Palazzo del Quirinale (4)** *(P.za del Quirinale, 06-469.91, www.quirinale.it; hours: Su 8:30AM–12PM)*, where, in the piazza fronting the palace, you'll find Roman copies of 5th-century BC Greek statues of the brothers Castor and Pollux. Known for their equestrian abilities, they are always represented, as here, with lively horses. The Palazzo was built in the 16th century by Pope Gregory XIII as a summer residence for the pope and his entourage.

Sober, dignified 19th-century **Piazza della Repubblica (5)** was built on what was the *exedra*, the semicircular recess, of the Baths of Diocletian. It was constructed during the 19th-century redevelopment that marked Rome's new status as capital of Italy. Elegant colonnades encircle the piazza and the central fountain with four bronze nymphs astride various water animals. The naked nymphs created a scandal in 1901 when they were unveiled.

Across the piazza are the Baths of Diocletian, or **Terme di Diocleziano (6)** *(Viale E. de Nicola 79, 06-39.96.77.00, archeoroma.beniculturali.it/en/museums; hours: Tu–Su 9AM–7:45PM)*. Built by the forced labor of 40,000 Christians, the grounds included gardens, galleries, concert halls, libraries, and the bathhouse, which held 3,000 people at a time. After the Ostrogoths demolished the aqueducts, the baths were abandoned in 538, and ten centuries later Pope Pius IV commissioned the 86-year-old Michelangelo to convert the ruins into a church, **Santa Maria degli Angeli (11)** *(see page 81)*. With the city's restoration projects of 2000, the Terme became part of the **Museo Nazionale di Roma (10)** *(see page 81)*.

Arts & Entertainment:

The gallery at the **San Luca National Academy of Art (7)** *(P.za dell'Accademia di San Luca 77, 06-679.88.50, www.accademiasanluca.it; call for hours)* contains significant work by famous artists, such as Raphael and Canova. For a change of pace, check out the **Pasta Museum (8)** *(P.za Scanderbeg 117, 06-699.11.20, www.pastainmuseum.com; hours: daily 9:30AM–5:30PM)*.

It contains whatever you want to know about pasta, and more—history, production, and pasta-themed art. Take Via di San Vincenzo, which eventually becomes the beautiful Via della Pilotta, to **Palazzo Colonna (9)** *(Via della Pilotta 17, 06-678.43.50, www.galleriacolonna.it; hours: Sa 9AM–1:15PM, private visits by appt, closed Aug)*. The Colonna family mansion was begun in the 15th century by Pope Martin V Colonna but finished in the 18th century. The family's art collection is open to the public in the art gallery, from where you can see the lovely private gardens and ruins of the Temple of Serapis.

The museum at the Baths of Diocletian, **Museo Nazionale di Roma: Terme di Diocleziano (10)** *(Via Enrico de Nicola 79, 06-39.96.77.00, archeoroma.beniculturali.it/en/museums; hours: Tu–Su 9AM–7:45PM)*, affords a marvelous view of the ancient Roman site and the central cloister, restored by Michelangelo. Fragments of the baths are in **Santa Maria degli Angeli (11)** *(P.za della Repubblica, 06-488.08.12, www.santamariadegliangeliroma.it; hours: daily 7AM–6:30PM)*, the magnificent church designed by Michelangelo. The restored **Aula Ottagona (12)** *(Via Romita 8, 06-39.96.77.00; hours: Tu–Su 9AM–7:45PM)* now exhibits large classical sculptures.

If you haven't had enough drama, take in a great Italian operatic tragedy at **Teatro dell'Opera (13)** *(P.za Beniamino Gigli 7, 06-481.601, box office 06-481.70.03, www.operaroma.it; box office hours: Tu–Sa 9AM–5PM, Su 9AM–1:30PM; tickets online: Opera site or www.listicket.it)*. Or check out the old stables and coach house of the presidential palace, **Scuderie del Quirinale (14)** *(Via XXIV Maggio 16, 06-39.96.75.00, english.scuderiequirinale.it, www.scuderiequirinale.it; hours: Su–Th 10AM–8PM, F–Sa 10AM–10:30PM)*, revamped and turned into a cultural center and exhibition space by architect Gae Aulenti. Another arts center in the area, **Palazzo delle Esposizioni (15)** *(Via Nazionale 194, 06-48.94.11, info & box office 06-39.96.75.00, www.palaexpo.it; hours: Tu–Th, Su 10AM–8PM, F–Sa 10AM–10:30PM)*, is an exciting forum for contemporary art, including cinema and photography.

PLACES TO EAT & DRINK
Where to Eat:

Whether or not you love beer, **L'Antica Birreria Peroni (16)** (€–€€) *(Via San Marcello 19, 06-679.53.10, www.anticabirreriaperoni.it; hours: M–Sa 12PM–12AM)* is an experience in social eating. The communal seating integrates you with the Roman beer hall scene. The Tyrolean menu is hearty, and the beers are exceptional. Great service, great food, and a friendly welcome greet you at **Trattoria Tritone (17)** (€€) *(Via dei Maroniti 1, 06-679.81.81, www.trattoriatritone.com; hours: daily 12PM–11PM)*, where you can hobnob with Italian journalists. **Il Gelato di San Crispino (18)** (€) *(Via della Panetteria 42, 06-679.39.24, www.ilgelatodisancrispino.it; hours: Su–Th 12PM–12:30AM, F–Sa 12PM–1:30AM, closed Tu in autumn/winter)* is possibly the best ice cream shop in all Rome. The ingredients are so fresh and seasonal that some of the flavors come and go in less than a month.

Bars & Nightlife:

The oldest wine shop in Rome has a wine bar next door: cozy **Trimani (19)** *(Via Cernaia 37b, 06-446.96.30, www.trimani.com; call for hours)*, near the Baths of Diocletian, offers a wide variety of wines and good food.

WHERE TO SHOP

One of Italy's largest chain bookstores, **Feltrinelli International (20)** *(Via Vittorio Emanuele Orlando 78-81, 06-482.78.78, 06-487.09.99, 06-487.01.71/83, www.lafeltrinelli.it; hours: M–Sa 9AM–8PM, Su 10:30AM–1:30PM, 4PM–8PM, closed Su in Aug)* carries a large selection of books, CDs, and DVDs in their original language, including English. The selection of wines and gourmet foods at **Trimani (21)** *(Via Goito 20, 06-446.96.61, www.trimani.com; hours: M–Sa 9AM–8:30PM)* is fantastic. Sample the olive oil before you buy. Purchase a jar of truffle paste, bread, and a bottle of Chianti for a picnic at nearby Baths of Diocletian. The ceramics at **Il Giardino di Domenico Persiani (22)** *(Via Torino 92, 06-488.38.86)* will fill you with delight. Ready-made tiles, special order pieces, copies of famous statues—you could spend an afternoon browsing through the garden.

WHERE TO STAY

Hotel Exedra (23) (€€€) *(P.za della Repubblica 47, 06-48.93.81, www.boscolohotels.com)* integrates ancient and modern. Glass floors in meeting rooms allow viewing of Roman ruins. The atrium is airy and light. Rooms are spacious. The **St. Regis Grand (24)** (€€€-€€€€) *(Via Vittorio Emanuele Orlando 3, 06-47.091, www.stregisrome.com, www.starwoodhotels.com)* lives up to its name. Elegant Murano chandeliers set the tone, and every room has frescoes above the bed. **Residenza Cellini (25)** (€-€€) *(Via Modena 5, 06-47.82.52.04, www.residenzacellini.it)*, a B&B run by two brothers and a sister, has large rooms with hardwood floors, high ceilings, and bathrooms with hydromassage showers and heated towel racks. Offering value and convenience, B&B **Flowerome (26)** (€) *(Via Filippo Turati 23, 033-55.63.77.03, http://flowerome.net)* is just a few minutes from the Termini and within walking distance to many historic sites.

ESQUILINO & MONTI

B: *Santa Maria Maggiore*—16, 70, 71, 714;
San Pietro in Vincoli—75, 84, 117

M: *A or B to Termini; B to Cavour;
A to Vittorio Emanuele*

• SNAPSHOT •

The area of Esquilino and Monti once included both the most prosperous and the most wretched of Rome's inhabitants. Esquilino Hill, southeast of the Quirinale, was home to the wealthiest families of ancient and papal Rome, while Monti, the low, swampy slum between the two hills, was left to the urban poor. Today Monti is one of the trendiest areas of Rome, with some great restaurants, numerous interesting shops, and designers and craftsmen who ply their trade with the passion of their spiritual forefathers.

Esquilino has become Rome's experiment in multiculturalism. In a city not especially known for diversity, recent immigrants have made this area a colorful mix of cultures from many continents. Ethiopians, Eritreans, Chinese, and Italians coexist and thrive, with shops and businesses exchanging services and clients. One of Rome's most magnificent churches is located in Esquilino: Santa Maria Maggiore is superb, both architecturally and artistically. San Pietro in Vincoli, another must-see, contains Michelangelo's *Moses*.

PLACES TO SEE
Landmarks:

One of Rome's great basilicas, ★**SANTA MARIA MAGGIORE (27)** *(P.za di Santa Maria Maggiore, 06-48.31.95, 06-69.88.68.00, www.vatican.va; hours: daily 7AM–6:45PM)* is an archi- tectural marvel, successfully integrating several different styles—Romanesque, medieval, Renaissance, and Baroque—with front and rear façades on two large piaz- zas. The legend of its creation is that the Virgin Mary came to Pope Liberius in a dream, instructing him to build a church in a place where he found snow. On August 5, 356, it snowed on the Esquiline. Seeing this as a miracle, Pope Liberius obeyed her exhortation. In a yearly service commemorating the event, white rose petals are dropped from the church's ceiling. The interi- or is amazing. Gilded coffered ceilings; opulent chapels; magnificent detailing in marble, bronze, and porphyry; and spectacular mosaics are among the wonders of Santa Maria Maggiore, which is one of the four major basilicas of Rome (along with St. Peter's in the Vatican, San Giovanni in Laterano, and San Paolo Fuori le Mura).

The chains that bound St. Peter in Jerusalem and while he was in the Mamertine Prison near the Roman Forum *(see page 129)* are the relics that give ★**SAN PIETRO IN VINCOLI (28)** *(P.za di San Pietro in Vincoli 4A, 06-488.28.65, 06-97.84.49.52; hours: daily 8AM–12:30PM, 3:30PM–6:30PM, Oct–Mar til 6PM)* its name ("St. Peter in Chains") and are displayed below

85

the high altar. Legend has it that when the chains were placed next to each other, they miraculously fused together. Originally built in the 5th century, the church has undergone many touch-ups and restorations. It is best known for **Michelangelo's masterpiece, *Moses*** , sculpted for the tomb of Pope Julius II. The seated figure instills reverence and embodies wisdom, fortitude, honor, conviction, and inner strength. Interestingly, the horns on his head are the result of a flawed translation from the Old Testament. Instead of horns, they're supposed to be beams of light. In addition to *Moses*, Michelangelo is also believed to have finished the statues of *Rachel* and *Leah* before having to abandon this project to begin work on the Sistine Chapel.

Emperor Nero is said to have set fire to Rome in AD 64, perhaps to grab most of the Oppian Hill and build the **Domus Aurea (29)** *(Via della Domus Aurea, 06-39.96.77.00, archeoroma.beniculturali.it/siti-archeologici; currently closed due to nearby tunnel collapse)*. Encircled by man-made lakes and forests, his "Golden House," a palace fit for Nero's megalomania and debauchery, was 25 times as big as the Colosseum and was covered in gold outside and inlaid with jewels and mother-of-pearl inside. The ruins of the **Domus Aurea (29)** are situated in the lovely park on the Oppian side of the Esquilino. The **Parco del Colle Oppio (30)** is as high as the top floors of the Colosseum; thus, the ancient amphitheatre seems to rise up so close you could almost touch it.

Arts & Entertainment:
Galleria Termini/GATE (31) *(Termini Station, Ala Mazzoniana, Via Giolitti 34, by gate/binario 24, 06-47.84.13.93, 06-06.08; hours: Oct–Mar W–M 9:30AM–8:30PM, Apr–Sep W–M 10:30AM–9:30PM)* exhibits modern art and photography, providing a great way to pass the time while waiting for your train.

PLACES TO EAT & DRINK
Where to Eat:
Agata e Romeo (32) (€€€€) *(Via Carlo Alberto 45, 06-446.61.15, www.agataeromeo.it; hours: M, Sa 8PM–11PM, Tu–F 12:30PM–2:30PM, 8PM–11PM)* is on everyone's list: Roman haute cuisine with classic underpinnings. Eating is a trip here, the comfortable but subdued décor bowing out to focus the senses on the food. Sheep's milk cheese tart with pear sauce, celery and oxtail terrine, pasta with saffron cheese, Icelandic cod—they're all distinctive and excellent.

F.I.S.H. (33) (€€) *(Via dei Serpenti 16, 06-47.82.49.62, www.f-i-s-h.it; hours: Tu–Su 7PM–12AM)* stands for Fine International Seafood House, and that's exactly what it is. From sushi and sashimi to the most delicate, thin fish *carpaccios*, the menu is a fantasy from the sea with Mediterranean, Asian, and Pacific Rim cuisine. A restaurant that's made its mark in the Monti area with exceptional Japanese food is **Hasekura (34)** (€€-€€€) *(Via dei Serpenti 27, 06-48.36.48, www.hasekura.it; hours: daily 12PM–2:30PM, 7PM–10:30PM)*, one of the hottest eateries around.

Bars & Nightlife:
Al Vino Al Vino (35) *(Via dei Serpenti 19, 06-48.58.03; hours: daily 10:30AM–2:30PM, 5PM–1AM)* is mostly a wine bar frequented by a multiculti crowd, a great place to check out the local hipsters. It has a good selection of wines, especially sweet wines *(passiti)*, and a variety of *grappas*. The crowd at **Bohemien (36)** *(Via degli Zingari 36, 0339-722.46.22, www.colosseo.org/caffebohemien; hours: W–M 6PM–2AM)* is casual, friendly, and mostly gay; the bar is unpretentious and doubles as a design, art, and photography bookstore. Romans adore **Fiddler's Elbow (37)** *(Via dell'Olmata 43, 06-487.21.10, www.thefiddlerselbow.com; hours: daily 5PM–1:30AM)*, an old Irish pub whose fiddlers, all volunteer musicians, might inspire you to dance an impromptu *céil'*.

WHERE TO SHOP

With more than 80 varieties of bread, **Panella (38)** *(Via Merulana 54-55, 06-487.24.35, www.panella-artedelpane.it; hours: M–Sa 8AM–12AM, Su 8:30AM–4PM)* has more than enough varieties to satisfy your cravings. If chocolate is your thing, **La Bottega del Cioccolato (39)** *(Via Leonina 82, 06-482.14.73, www.labottegadelcioccolato.it)* is an obligatory stop. The dark chocolate, 90% cocoa (Brazilian), is amazing, but the truffles, peppermint bars, and fruit and nut combinations are all divine. Fashionistas, don't miss **Le Gallinelle (40)** *(Via del Boschetto 76, 06-48.44.50, www.legallinelle.it)*, a boutique that carries its own creations. Owner Wilma Silvestri makes draped evening gowns, sundresses, and more. A vintage Gucci bag might be just the thing for a night out in Monti. On the north side of the Esquilino, not far from the Baths of Diocletian, is the **Termini Train Station (41)** *(P.za del Cinquecento, www.romatermini. com)*. In the city's perennial attempts to brighten the seedy area, a mini-mall was created here in 2000, with shops, boutiques, bookstores, eateries, and an art gallery *(see page 87)*, as well as a 24-hour supermarket. Despite this resurrection, the train station is still to be avoided at night. The watchmakers at **L'Artigianaio Orologi (42)** *(Via Urbana 103, 06-474.22.84, call for hours)* specialize in sales and repair of vintage timepieces.

WHERE TO STAY

Radisson Blu es (43) (€€-€€€) *(Via Filippo Turati 171, 06-44.48.41, reservations 06-44.48.47.00, www.radisson blu.com)* is the cat's meow in high-tech, minimalist living. Often a venue for fashion and film shoots, it includes a state-of-the-art gym, rooftop pool, spa, ultra-modern restaurant **Sette**, and cocktail bar **Zest**. For studio or apartment rentals, **Residenza Monti (44)** (€-€€) *(Via dei Serpenti 15, 06-481.57.36, www.therelaxing hotels.com)* provides a quiet respite from the buzz of the Monti district. The rooms are rather small but comfortable. Bare beams and iron beds give **Antica Locanda (45)** (€) *(Via del Boschetto 84, 06-48.48.94, www.antica-locanda.com)* a special charm. Its roof garden overlooks ancient ruins.

SAN LORENZO

B: 71, 204, 310, 492, 649
M: A or B to Termini

• SNAPSHOT •

San Lorenzo is a lively district with a left-wing, antifascist past. Created in the late 19th century, the working-class neighborhood suffered from substandard living conditions, and the populace rebelled. By the 1920s, they were battling fascists in the streets; during Mussolini's era San Lorenzo became a meeting place for antifascists. Ironically, it was heavily bombed during World War II; consequently the buildings are post-1945 constructions. Currently, the district is fascinating because of the artistic passion and cultural diversity of its inhabitants; it is home to a young generation of artists. Residents, along with students from the nearby university, La Sapienza, and visitors coming to experience the innovative and creative energy of the district, keep the bars, clubs, and eateries open all night. The old Cerere pasta factory has been converted into artists' lofts. With

the influx of young designers, hip restaurants and bars have followed, sharing the streets with traditional, inexpensive working-class trattorias. San Lorenzo has no real landmarks of note; rather, it is interesting because of its creative life force.

PLACES TO SEE
Landmarks:

La Sapienza *(Piazzale Aldo Moro 5, 06-499.11, www.uniroma1.it)* is the largest university in Europe, and its main campus, **Città Universitaria**, is just north of the San Lorenzo district. The university's architecture is typical of the fascist aesthetic of the 1930s, when it was built. At the quarter's northern tip on Piazzale del Verano, the basilica of **San Lorenzo fuori le Mura (46)** *(Piazzale del Verano 3, 06-49.15.11/06-446.61.84, www.basilicasanlorenzo.it; hours: Apr–Sept daily 7:30AM– 12:30PM, Oct–Mar daily 7:30AM–12:30PM, 3PM–7PM)* was originally a gift from Emperor Constantine to house the tomb of St. Lawrence. Byzantine icons, created with pieces of marble in the Greek tradition, lack the brilliance evident in Roman mosaics made of glass.

Arts & Entertainment:

San Lorenzo has increasingly become a hotbed of contemporary art. Blending into the ethos of the neighborhood, **Galleria Pino Casagrande (47)** *(Via degli Ausoni 7a, 06-446.34.80, www.pino casagrande.com; hours: M–F 5PM– 8PM)*, in the textile connoisseur's home, displays his art collection.

Furniture by Mies van der Rohe, Le Corbusier, Ettore Sottsass, and others blends with the antiquities and contemporary art that Casagrande has collected, including works by Sol Le Witt, Donald Judd, and Julian Opie.

PLACES TO EAT & DRINK
Where to Eat:

San Lorenzo would be worth a visit if only to taste the fabulous southern Italian cuisine at **Vinosteria (48) (€€)** *(Via dei Sabelli 51, 06-494.07.26; hours: daily 7:30PM–1AM)*. Delicate flavors blend to burst on the palate. Leave room for the chocolate soufflé. Casual **Formula 1 (49) (€)** *(Via degli Equi 13, 06-445.38.66, hours: M–Sa 7PM–closing, no lunch, closed Aug)* packs in students and locals for its yummy pizzas and low prices.

Filmmaker Pier Paolo Pasolini, who loved working-class San Lorenzo, was a regular at **Pommidoro (50) (€€)** *(P.za dei Sanniti 44, 06-445.26.52; call for hours)*. Local artists continue to cross its threshold, as well as Roma team soccer stars. The *spaghetti alla carbonara* is great, and the place is known for its grilled meats. The friendly owner might be prompted to tell you stories about the neighborhood. One of the first eateries to open in San Lorenzo, **Tram Tram (51) (€€)** *(Via dei Reti 44, 06-49.04.16, www.tramtram.it; hours: Tu–Su 12:30PM–3:30PM, 7:30PM–11:30PM)* continues to be exceptionally good. Beans with chicory, swordfish with anchovies—the combinations are unique and delicious. The place gets its name from the area's tramline; old train pieces serve as booths and wine racks.

Bars & Nightlife:

The wine bar **Ferrazza (52)** *(Via dei Volsci 59, 06-49.05.06; hours: M–Sa 6PM–2AM)* is one of the city's best drinking spots. Enjoy people-watching amid crowds of young artists, local artisans, and students. It has a selection of fabulous cocktail snacks in the early evening. The cavernlike interior is brick-lined and pleasant.

WHERE TO SHOP

The working-class roots of San Lorenzo can be seen in the artisan workshops, open-air markets, and neighborly relations among the locals. The leather goods at **Claudio Sano (53)** *(Largo degli Osci 67a, 06-446.92.84, www.claudiosano.it)*, all handmade on the premises, are beautifully crafted from carefully treated and finished leather. Imaginative designs for handbags, briefcases, sandals, belts, and other products assure the unique look of these goods. The creative jewelry designs of Myriam Bottazzi, available at her showroom **Aspecifico Atelier Myriam B (54)** *(Via degli Ausoni 7, 06-44.36.13.05, www.myriamb.it; hours: Tu–Sa 11AM–8PM, M 4PM–8PM)* have become legendary. They make a statement without being excessive. Fashion designers Romeo Gigli and Martine Sitbon are among her clients.

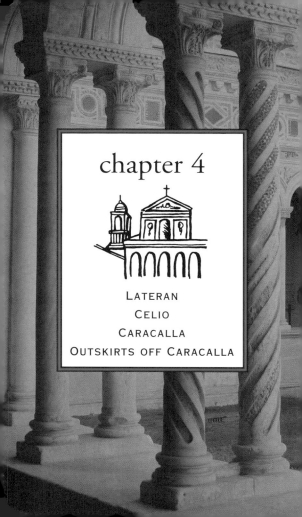

chapter 4

LATERAN
CELIO
CARACALLA
OUTSKIRTS OFF CARACALLA

LATERAN
CELIO
CARACALLA
OUTSKIRTS OFF CARACALLA

Places to See:
1. San Giovanni in Laterano
2. Piazza di San Giovanni in Laterano
3. Scala Santa
4. Santa Croce in Gerusalemme
5. Porta Maggiore
6. Santi Quattro Coronati
7. Museum of Musical Instruments
8. Historic Museum of the Liberation of Rome
15. San Clemente
16. Case Romane del Celio
17. Clivio di Scauro
18. San Gregorio Magno
19. Villa Celimontana
20. Santa Maria in Domnica
21. Santo Stefano Rotondo
22. Galleria Arte e Pensieri
23. Antiquarium Comunale
24. Galleria SALES
37. Santa Balbina
38. Santi Nereo e Achilleo
39. San Sisto Vecchio
40. San Cesareo
41. San Giovanni a Porta Latina
42. San Giovanni in Oleo
43. BATHS OF CARACALLA ★
44. Columbarium of Pomponius Hylas
45. Scipio Tomb
46. Porta San Sebastiano
47. Wall Museum
48. Arch of Drusus
49. Gruppo Storico Romano
50. Appian Way
51. Catacombs of San Callisto
52. Catacombs of San Sebastiano
53. Fosse Ardeatine
54. Catacombs of Domitilla
55. Tomb of Cecilia Metella

Places to Eat & Drink:
9. Ai Tre Scalini
10. Isidoro
11. Pizzeria Luzzi
25. Crab
26. Naumachia
27. Centrum
28. Café Café
29. Coming Out

★ *Top Picks*

Where to Shop:
12. Dierre Bijoux
13. Soul Food
14. Via Sannio
30. Harmonia Mundi
32. Arte Colosseo
33. Gutenberg al Colosseo

Where to Stay:
34. Hotel Capo d'Africa
35. Hotel Lancelot
36. Palazzo Manfredi

LATERAN

B: P.za San Giovanni—16, 81, 85, 87, 186, 650, 850; Santa Croce in Gerusalemme—16, 81, 649, 810

M: A to Manzoni or San Giovanni; B to Colosseo

• SNAPSHOT •

The area of Lateran lies between the Celian and Esquiline hills. It was named after a wealthy family, the Laterani. Today the Lateran is known for the basilica of Rome, San Giovanni in Laterano (St. John Lateran), which was founded in the 4th century AD by Emperor Constantine. He had a vision before going into battle: Christ came to him and told him to put a Christian symbol on his soldiers' shields. Constantine won the battle against Maxentius, thereby becoming emperor. He converted to the new religion and immediately legalized Christianity, forbidding the persecution of its followers. Most people in Rome, however, were still non-Christians, so he chose a location away from the center of the city to build a basilica—in the Lateran. It was less likely to agitate the pagans, but was still within the walls of Rome.

PLACES TO SEE
Landmarks:
The focus of this quarter is **San Giovanni in Laterano (1)** (P.za

97

di San Giovanni in Laterano 4, 06-69.88.63.92, Museum 06-69.88.64.09, www.vatican.va; hours: Church daily 7AM–6:30PM, Cloister daily 9AM–6PM, Museum daily 10AM–5:30PM), the cathedral of Rome. It was built by Emperor Constantine in the early 4th century over the barracks of Emperor Maxentius's bodyguards, thus symbolically proclaiming Constantine's victory over Maxentius and the victory of Christianity over paganism. Architecturally modified over the years, the present church dates from the 17th century. It is one of the four major basilicas of Rome, together with St. Peter's in the Vatican, Santa Maria Maggiore, and San Paolo Fuori le Mura. Its façade, with 15 stunningly enormous statues standing on the pediment atop the church, makes the basilica recognizable from a distance. Inside, the statues of the twelve apostles were sculpted by Borromini.

The cathedral's **Baptistery** and the **Lateran Palace**, the old papal residence, are on the **Piazza di San Giovanni in Laterano (2)**, facing another Egyptian obelisk, the oldest and tallest in Rome. The profusion of Egyptian obelisks in Rome attests to the military might of ancient Rome: they were highly prized war trophies because of their power in Egypt as symbols of the pharaohs' immortality and divinity. Every May 1, labor unions celebrate International Workers' Day on the piazza with a free rock concert.

On the eastern edge of the piazza is what is thought to be a relic brought to Rome in 326 from the Holy Land by St. Helena, mother of Emperor Constantine. The

Scala Santa (3) *(P.za di San Giovanni in Laterano 14, 06-772.66.41, www.scalasanta.org; hours: daily 6:30AM–12PM, 3:30PM–6PM)*, the Holy Staircase, is comprised of 28 marble stairs said to be the very steps Christ climbed in Pontius Pilate's palace in Jerusalem before his crucifixion. No foot is allowed to touch them, so they are covered by wooden boards which pious Christians ascend on their knees.

In the eastern sector of the Lateran, **Santa Croce in Gerusalemme (4)** *(P.za di Santa Croce in Gerusalemme 12, 06-7061.3053, www.santacroceroma.it; hours: daily 7AM–12:45PM, 3:30PM–7:30PM)* (Holy Cross in Jerusalem) was part of St. Helena's palace. Built in 320 to house relics of the Crucifixion that she was said to have brought back from Jerusalem, it was redone in the 18th century. It houses what are supposed to be pieces of Christ's cross (the "True Cross"), a nail from the cross, two thorns from the Crown of Thorns, and the finger that doubting St. Thomas purportedly put into Christ's wound.

A few streets to the north, **Porta Maggiore (5)** *(P.za di Porta Maggiore)*, with its two arches, was the entry point for aqueducts carrying water into the city. The original acqueduct, Aqua Claudia, was built by Emperor Claudius in AD 52. **Santi Quattro Coronati (6)** *(Via dei Santi Quattro Coronati 20, 06-70.47.54.27, www.santiquattrocoronati.org; hours: Church daily 6:30AM–12:45PM, 3PM–7:45PM)*, "Four Crowned Saints," is a convent dedicated to four Christian soldiers executed for refusing to renounce their religion. The 13th-century frescoes in the Chapel of St. Sylvester tell the story of Emperor Constantine suffering from the plague. Be sure not to miss the cloister *(ring the bell and make a donation to enter; hours: daily 10AM–11:45AM, 4PM–5:45PM)*, with its charming fountain and romantic arcades.

Arts & Entertainment:

The collection at the **Museum of Musical Instruments (7)** *(P.za Santa Croce in Gerusalemme 9A, 06-701.47.96, 06-32.810, www.galleriaborghese.it/nuove/estrumentiinfo.htm; hours: Tu–Su 8:30AM–7:30PM)* covers typically Italian pieces as well as wind, string, and percussion instruments from around the world and of all eras. The famous Barberini harp is part of the collection, as is one of the first pianos ever built, made in the early 18th century by the instrument's inventor, Bartolomeo Cristoforo. Considerably less charming is the **Historic Museum of the Liberation of Rome (8)** *(Via Tasso 145, 06-700.38.66, www.viatasso.eu; hours: Tu, Th, F 9:30AM–12:30PM, 3:30PM–7PM, W, Sa–Su 9:30AM–12:30PM)*, in a building that was the Gestapo's headquarters and prison during World War II. The museum honors, among others, the many antifascists who were interrogated, tortured, and jailed there.

PLACES TO EAT & DRINK
Where to Eat:

Ai Tre Scalini (9) (€€) *(Via dei Santi Quattro Coronati 30, 06-709.63.09, www.ai3scalini.com; call for hours, closed M)* offers creative Mediterranean dishes and a cozy atmosphere with a lovely outdoor eating area. **Isidoro (10)** (€) *(Via di San Giovanni in Laterano 59a, 06-*

700.82.66, www.hostariaisidoro.com; hours: Su–F 12PM–3PM, 7PM–2AM, Sa 7PM–2AM), a great pasta bar, mostly vegetarian, offers tastings of different pasta dishes at once.

WHERE TO SHOP

The father-son Ranati team at **Dierre Bijoux (12)** *(Via Merulana 165, 06-70.49.46.95)* makes great costume jewelry for fashion shows, movie stars, and the Miss Italia pageant. The Ranatis sell ready-made or custom-created paste. **Soul Food (13)** *(Via di San Giovanni in Laterano 192, 06-70.45.20.25, www.haterecords.com/html/soulfood.html; hours: Tu–Sa 10:30AM–1:30PM, 3:30PM–8PM)* stocks rare LPs and single records, both Italian and imported; it's not cheap, but vinyl freaks will have fun fishing for treasures. The flea market in **Via Sannio (14)** *(M–F 8AM–2PM, Sa 8AM–5PM)* has great buys in vintage, secondhand, and new clothes, with end-of-week sales. As with all flea markets, you need patience, but the payoff can be big if you find a fabulous bargain. And it's not as chaotic as **Porta Portese** *(see page 172)*.

101

CELIO

*B: 60, 75, 81, 175, 271, 673; San Clemente—
85, 87, 117, 186, 571, 810, 850;
Santo Stefano Rotondo—81, 117, 673*

M: B to Colosseo or Circo Massimo

• SNAPSHOT •

Tiers of historical eras, all critical to the development of Rome, are everywhere in evidence in the Celian Hill area. The foundations of the Temple of Claudius give a taste of what lies in the nearby Roman Forum. In the Celio *quartiere*, older Roman ruins gave way to early Christian edifices. Many of these, in turn, were reconstructed in medieval times, then again in the Baroque period. Over the centuries, pillaging hordes—Goths, Vandals, Saracens, and Normans, among others—slashed and burned Rome, and older civilizations gave way to newer ones. But the old ones weren't swept away; they simply formed the foundations of each succeeding era. Beautiful and oppressive, wondrous and gruesome, Rome never lets go of its past.

The Celian Hill is part of the Archaeological Zone and, as such, is serene and verdant. As you stroll through the green spaces and parks of the quarter, you'll forget the violence that gave Rome its power, but you'll

PLACES TO SEE
Landmarks:

The church of **San Clemente (15)** *(Via di San Giovanni in Laterano, 06-774.00.21, www.basilicasanclemente. com; hours: M–Sa 9AM– 12:30PM, 3PM–6PM, Su*

12PM–6PM) is an extraordinary example of the visible layers of history that have piled upon Rome, with a 12th-century church built on a 4th-century church, built on an ancient 2nd-century BC temple. The 12th-century medieval church is notable for its mosaics, frescoes, and dazzling examples of Cosmati work. In the lower level of the church lies the tomb of Pope Clement I, for whom the church is named.

Walking westward, you'll arrive at the green expanse of the Celio park and hill, dotted by ruins and bits of old walls and gateways, such as the **Arch of Dolabella** *(Via di San Paolo della Croce)*. A large portion of the green park was once the **Temple of Claudius**, built by Agrippina (Nero's mother) for her husband, Emperor Claudius, after she poisoned him. Some of the temple's ruins make up the foundation of the bell tower *(campanile)* of the church of **Santi Giovanni e Paolo**, while beneath the church is a fascinating subterranean complex of ancient Roman houses, the **Case Romane del Celio (16)** *(P.za Santi Giovanni e Paolo 13, Church: 06-700.57.45/06-*

772.711, Excavations: 06-70.45.45.44, www.case romane.it; hours: Excavations Th–M 10AM–1PM, 3PM–6PM). The church itself was built in the 4th century and dedicated to John and Paul, two of Constantine's Roman officers who converted to Christianity.

To the left of the church is **Clivio di Scauro (17)**, a picturesque 2nd-century BC street built by Roman magistrate Scauro. The street passes beneath the buttresses of the church, where you'll find the entrance to the excavations of ancient Roman houses. A fascinating maze of 20 rooms from four 1st-century AD buildings on various levels reveals spaces that were apparently used secretly for Christian worship in a time when that could cost you your head. Frescoes and traces of paintings also make this a worthwhile visit.

At the end of **Clivio di Scauro (17)** is an area dominated by **San Gregorio Magno (18)** *(P.za di San Gregorio Magno 1, 06-700.82.27, www.camaldolesiromani.it; hours: daily winter 9AM–12PM, 3PM–6PM, summer 9AM–1PM, 3PM–7:30PM)*, a 6th-century monastery converted by Pope Gregory I (St. Gregory the Great) from what used to be his home.

Much of the Celio is composed of **Villa Celimontana (19)** *(Via della Navicella, see also page 105)* and its park, belonging to the Dukes of Mattei from 1553 to 1928. The family villa is now the domain of the Italian Geographic Society and closed to the public. The formal gardens, however, are a beautiful public park dotted with various marble pieces from the Mattei collection. On the eastern edge of the park is **Santa Maria in Domnica (20)** *(P.za della Navicella 10, 06-77.20.26.85, www.santamariain domnica.it; hours: daily 8:30AM–12:30PM, 4:30PM–7PM)*, known colloquially as the *Navicella*, or "little boat," after the stone galley that stands outside it, which was most likely a temple offering made by a grateful Roman.

Across Via della Navicella and nearly opposite **Santa Maria in Domnica (20)** is Rome's oldest circular church, **Santo Stefano Rotondo (21)** *(Via di Santo Stefano Rotondo 7, 06-4211.9130/1, www.santo-stefano-rotondo.it; hours: Apr–Oct Tu–Su 9:30AM–12:30PM, 3PM–6PM, Nov–Mar Tu–Su 9:30AM–12:30PM, 2PM–5PM)*. Built in the 5th century, its Byzantine atmosphere of simplicity and spiritual contemplation is appealing, although the 16th-century frescoes are terrifying: images of martyrs being boiled in oil, flayed, torturously stretched, and having their hands chopped off are quite graphic.

Arts & Entertainment:

In June and July the **Alexanderplatz Jazz Festival** is held in the **Villa Celimontana (19)** *(see also page 104)* park, with evening concerts featuring major jazz musicians. An international crowd and jazz cognoscenti flock to hear the likes of Keith Jarrett, Lou Reed, and Roberto Gatto, among others.

The place to spot fresh talent is **Galleria Arte e Pensieri (22)** *(Via Ostilia 3a, 06-700.2404; hours: Th–Sa 4PM–8PM & by appt)*, an art collective which, besides showing four exhibitions annually, is a meeting place for up-and-coming and less-established artists. This is the place to check out when looking for the newest in contemporary art. The **Antiquarium Comunale (23)** *(Viale del Parco del Celio 22, 06-700.15.69; hours: summer M–Sa 9AM–7PM, Su 9AM–1PM, winter M–Sa 9AM–5PM, Su 9AM–1PM)* houses a collection of ancient tools and utensils used in the home as well as other artifacts. Check out **Galleria SALES (24)** *(Via dei Querceti 4-5, 06-77.59.11.22, www.galleriasales.it; hours: Tu–Sa 3:30PM–7:30PM, closed Aug)* for some of the best Italian, American, and British artists.

PLACES TO EAT & DRINK
Where to Eat:

In a street with remarkable hotels, **Crab (25)** (€€€-€€€€) *(Via Capo d'Africa 2, 06-77.20.36.36; hours: M, Sa 7:45PM–11:30PM, Tu–F 12:30PM–3:30PM, 7:45PM–11:30PM, closed Aug)* is an exceptional seafood restaurant; it's said to have the best oysters in the city, and a fashionable crowd fills the tables of this chic venue, which architect Terry Vaina remodeled out of an old warehouse. Much less expensive is **Naumachia (26)** (€-€€) *(Via Celimontana 7, 06-700.27.64, www.naumachiaroma.com; hours: daily 12PM–12AM)*, where you can enjoy traditional Roman cuisine in the brick-walled din-

ing room or outside with a view of ancient Rome. Besides pizzas and pastas, **Pizzeria Luzzi (€) (11)** *(Via San Giovanni in Laterano 88, at Via Celimontana, 06-709.6332)* does some excellent local dishes, such as *abbacchio alla Romana*, roast lamb.

In typical Roman style, it's friendly, noisy, busy, and cramped, and though the service might leave some people annoyed, it's a good cheap eat. The pizzas are delicious, as is the pasta *all'amatriciana*, a Roman dish. Locals love the authentic Roman pizzas at **Li Rioni (€)** *(Via dei Santi Quattro Coronati 24, 06-70.45.06.05; call for hours)*. The décor, reminiscent of an old Roman street, reflects the name, which in Roman dialect means "the neighborhoods." The pizzas are great; among the appetizers, don't miss the *carciofi alla romana* (Roman-style artichokes).

Bars & Nightlife:

Centrum (27) *(Hotel Capo d'Africa, Via Capo d'Africa 54, 06-77.28.01, www.hotelcapodafrica.com; call for hours)* is a hip, sleek bar in a hotel overlooking the Celio and the Colosseum. Though its specialties are whiskies and cigars, don't miss the cocktails of the *quartiere*, Caput Mundi and Colosseo. In an increasingly smart neighborhood, **Café Café (28)** *(Via dei Santi Quattro Coronati 44, 06-700.87.43, www.cafecafebistrot.it; hours: daily 10AM–1:30AM, Su brunch 11:30AM–4PM)* is a perfect place for a coffee, afternoon tea, late-night drinks, or an intimate *incontro*. It boasts a hearty wine list and sixty varieties of tea, and also offers soups, salads, and cheeses. The bar **Coming Out (29)** *(Via di San Giovanni in Laterano 8, 06-700.98.71, www.comingout.it; hours: daily 7AM–2AM)* is a gay hotspot with a fabulous view of the Colosseum. In warmer weather, the street in front fills up with a friendly crowd.

WHERE TO SHOP

Esoteric bookstore **Harmonia Mundi (30)** *(Via dei Santi Quattro Coronati 26/A, 06-70.47.68.34, www.harmoniamundi.it, hours: Tu–Su 10:30AM–7PM)* also sells candles and incense, and offers programs in meditation, longevity, and more. **Arte Colosseo (32)** *(Via di San Giovanni in Laterano 58, 06-709.64.04, www.artecolosseo.it; hours: Tu–Sa 10AM–7:30PM)* specializes in contemporary Italian paintings, original prints (some dating from the 17th century), and antique jewelry and watches. The bookstore **Gutenberg al Colosseo (33)** *(Via di San Giovanni in Laterano 112, 06-77.20.88.31, www.gutenbergantiqua.it)* focuses on classics and rare books going back as far as the 17th century. It also sells small framed prints of Rome through past centuries.

WHERE TO STAY

Hotel Capo d'Africa (34) (€€€) *(Via Capo d'Africa 54, 06-77.28.01, www.hotelcapodafrica.com)* is a stunning, high-design hotel studded with original art by contemporary Italian artists, such as Mariano Rossano and Paolo Canevari. The penthouse terrace, where breakfast is served, has a breathtaking view of the Celian Hill, the Colosseum, and the surrounding parks. Friendly and

understatedly elegant, **Hotel Lancelot (35) (€€)** *(Via Capo d'Africa 47, 06-70.45.06.15, www.lancelothotel.com)* is full of niches for quiet conversations or contemplative moments. The minimalist rooms and the lovely patio under an arbor of vines afford serenity in an area that has become abuzz with nightlife. Rooms at **Palazzo Manfredi (36)** (€€€€) *(Via Labicana 125, 06-77.59.13.80, www.palazzomanfredi.com)* have views of the ruins; suites look out onto the Colosseum. The interior design is appropriate for the quarter, with classical imitations and mosaics. The terrace at sunset is fabulous.

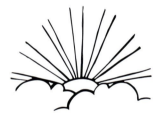

CARACALLA

B: Terme di Caracalla—160, 628;
Columbarium and tombs—218, 360, 628;
Porta San Sebastiano—218, 360

M: B to Circo Massimo

• SNAPSHOT •

The central focus of the vast green area south of the Celio is the 3rd-century *Terme di Caracalla* (Baths of Caracalla). The largest public bath and entertainment center until Diocletian built his baths, the *Terme di Caracalla* is now an impressive set of ruins, with arches, doorways, and platforms that conjure images of a time when Romans rubbed elbows in waters warmed by the sun-baked marble. Keeping fit was important to the ancients: bathing and exercise attended to physical well-being while libraries and areas for meetings and discussions kept the mind fit. Today, visitors to Rome can stay fit by strolling through the Caracalla complex or walking the road that marks the beginning of the ancient Appian Way. The Caracalla area is dotted with numerous medieval churches, but the other splendid feature of the quarter is the Aurelian Wall, a very large section of which is standing and in good condition.

> You must pay a fee to enter the Baths of Caracalla. Combination tickets with other site locations are available. You can visit the baths, as well as the Colosseum and the Palatine, for a fixed price. Visit or call for tickets: *Via di San Gregorio 30* and near the Arch of Titus on *Via Sacra (Roman Forum), 06-39.96.77.00.*

PLACES TO SEE
Landmarks:

While the **Baths of Caracalla (43)** *(details next page)* and the **Aurelian Wall** are the most majestic of the landmarks in Caracalla, a number of medieval churches mark the area's verdant landscape. Frescoes, mosaics, bell towers, and other features distinguish the churches of **Santa Balbina (37)** *(P.za di Santa Balbina 8, 06-578.02.07; hours: M–W, F 12:30PM–1PM, Th, Su 10:30AM–11:30AM)*, **Santi Nereo e Achilleo (38)** *(Via delle Terme di Caracalla 28, 06-575.79.96; hours: W–M 10AM–12PM, 4PM–6PM)*, **San Sisto Vecchio (39)** *(Piazzale Numa Pompilio 8, 06-77.20.51.74; hours: daily 9AM–11AM)*, **San Cesareo (40)** *(Via di Porta San Sebastiano, 06-58.23.01.40; hours: Su 9AM–12:15PM, & by appt.)*, **San Giovanni a Porta Latina (41)** *(Via di Porta Latina 17, 06-77.40.00.32, 06-70.47.59.38, www.sangiovanniaportalatina.it; hours: daily 7:30AM–12:30PM, 3PM–7PM)*, and **San Giovanni in Oleo (42)** *(Via di Porta Latina; ask at San Giovanni a Porta Latina)*. The latter (St. John in Oil) marks the spot where St. John the Evangelist was said to have been immersed in boiling oil, but emerged from the cauldron unharmed.

111

The ★**BATHS OF CARACALLA (43)** *(Viale delle Terme di Caracalla 52, 06-39.96.77.00; hours: M 9AM–2PM, Tu–Su 9AM–4:30PM, last entry 1 hr before closing)* were built in the early 3rd century and used for more than three centuries. The *Terme* accommodated 1,600 people in the baths and gyms at any time. The gyms were more "stretch-ariums" than workout rooms for gladiators, but they served the dual purpose of keeping people physically agile and providing meeting grounds for socializing. The bathing routine followed a specified order: after the changing rooms, it was first the *laconicum* (sauna), then a series of variously heated rooms, from *caldarium* (hot) to *tepidarium* (lukewarm) to *frigidarium* (you get the idea), and finally the *natatio*, the open-air swimming pool. Greek and Latin libraries, conference rooms, art galleries, and gardens rounded out the possibilities. Beneath this enormous complex was a network of rooms and tunnels where slaves maintained the workings of the baths. They ran on treadmill wheels that pumped water to the baths and stoked the fires of ovens that heated rooms through pipes in the walls and floors. When the Goths sacked Rome in 537, they destroyed the aqueducts supplying water, and the baths fell into disrepair. Until recently, operas were held in the open air at the Baths of Caracalla (*Aida* was famously staged with live camels and horses), but archaeologists have deemed the performances too stressful to the ancient structure.

The area is also noted for tombs and columbaria, or communal tombs. The columbaria were usually built by wealthy Romans to bury the ashes of their slaves and freedmen. In the southeastern part of Caracalla are the **Columbarium of Pomponius Hylas (44)** *(Via di Porta Latina 10; special permit needed to visit this site: contact 06-06.08 for details, guided tours 06-27.80.07.85)*, with their rows of niches. These were sold to people not wealthy enough to build their own tombs. The **Scipio Tomb (45)** *(Via di Porta San Sebastiano 9, 06-06.08, by appt)* contains copies of the sarcophagi (stone coffins), statues, and terra cotta funerary urns of a family of generals. The originals are in the Vatican Museums.

The **Via di Porta San Sebastiano** is the upper part of the old Appian Way. It leads to the **Aurelian Wall** and the **Porta San Sebastiano (46)** *(Via di Porta San Sebastiano 18)*. The wall and its gateways, impressive feats of ancient civil engineering, were created by Emperor Aurelian in the 3rd century to protect the city when Rome began to expand beyond the then existing walls. **Porta San Sebastiano (46)** is the spectacular gateway of the **Aurelian Wall**. Tall marble blocks form the foundation for the tall battlements. You can go up the towers, which house the **Wall Museum (47)** *(see page 114)*, and walk along the walls; the view is superb. In front of the gateway is the **Arch of Drusus (48)** *(Via di Porta San Sebastiano)*, which once supported the aqueduct channeling water to the Baths of Caracalla. While the entire **Aurelian Wall** is remarkable, the section between Porta San Sebastiano and Porta Latina is especially magnificent.

Arts & Entertainment:

The **Wall Museum (47)** *(Porta San Sebastiano, Via di Porta San Sebastiano 18, 06-70.47.52.84, 06-06.08, en.museodellemuraroma.it; hours: Tu–Su 9AM–2PM)* is dedicated to the history of Rome's containment walls, with prints and models as illustrations. If you have a desire to learn about the art of gladiator fighting and how to wield a sword, you can take lessons at the nearby **Gruppo Storico Romano (49)** *(Via Appia Antica 18, 06-51.60.79.51, www.gsr-roma.com)*.

> Because Caracalla is an area dedicated to ancient and medieval sites, for restaurants, bars, shops, and hotels try the Lateran or Celio *(see pages 97 and 102)* or the Aventine *(see page 143)*.

OUTSKIRTS OFF CARACALLA

Take a Bus Back Through Time
The Archeobus *(06-684.09.01/800-281.281, www.trambusopen.com)* leaves every hour from Termini Station and goes to the Baths of Caracalla, then takes **Via Appia Antica** to the catacombs and most of the sites listed below. You can get on and off at will. There are several stops worth checking out.

Appian Way (50)
(Via Appia Antica)

Catacombs of San Callisto (51)
(Via Appia Antica 126, 06-513.01.51, www.catacombe.roma.it; hours: Th–Tu 9AM–12PM, 2PM–5PM, closed Feb)

Catacombs of San Sebastiano (52)
(Via Appia Antica 136, 06-785.03.50, www.catacombe.org; hours: M–Sa 10AM–5PM)

Fosse Ardeatine (53)
(Via Ardeatina 174, 06-513.67.42; hours: M–F 8:15AM–3:30PM, Sa, Su 8:15AM–4:30PM)

Catacombs of Domitilla (54)
(Via delle Sette Chiese 282, 06-511.03.42, www.domitilla.info; hours: W–M 9AM–12PM, 2PM–5PM)

Tomb of Cecilia Metella (55)
(Via Appia Antica 161, 06-39.96.77.00, 06-06.08; hours: Tu–Su 9AM–4:30PM)

chapter 5

CAPITOLINE/CAMPIDOGLIO
FORUM & COLOSSEUM
PALATINE

CAPITOLINE/CAMPIDOGLIO FORUM & COLOSSEUM PALATINE

Places to See:
1. Palazzo Venezia
2. San Marco
3. Il Vittoriano
4. Santa Maria in Aracoeli
5. Aracoeli Stairway
6. Cordonata
7. Piazza del Campidoglio
8. Palazzo Senatorio
9. CAPITOLINE MUSEUMS ★
10. Temple of Jupiter
11. Tarpeian Rock
12. Museum of Palazzo Venezia
14. Trajan's Column
15. Trajan's Markets
16. Forum of Julius Caesar
17. Mamertine Prison
18. Forum of Augustus
19. Forum of Nerva
20. Arch of Septimius Severus
21. Curia
22. Temple of Saturn
23. Rostra
24. Basilica Julia
25. Temple of Castor and Pollux
26. Arch of Titus
27. Temple of Antonius and Faustina
28. Temple of Romulus
29. Basilica of Constantine and Maxentius
30. Temple of Vesta
31. House of the Vestal Virgins
32. Antiquarium Forense
33. Santa Francesca Romana
34. Arch of Constantine
35. COLOSSEUM ★
39. Farnese Gardens
40. Cryptoporticus
41. House of Livia
42. Temple of Cybele
43. Huts of Romulus
44. Domus Flavia
45. Domus Augustana
46. Stadium
47. Domus Septimius Severus
48. Palatine Museum

Places to Eat & Drink:
13. Caffè Capitolino
36. Ristorante Mario's

Where to Stay:
37. Fori Imperiali Cavalieri
38. Hotel Forum

★ *Top Picks*

The Capitoline, the Forum, and the Palatine are areas of concentrated archaeological and historical sites. Therefore, most restaurants in these areas are tourist traps or fast food joints. Some exceptions are noted. Otherwise, it's advisable to dine in districts nearby. For restaurants, bars, shops, and hotels near the Capitoline, turn to areas such as the Pantheon or Ghetto *(see pages 40 and 46)*, the Quirinale or Monti *(see pages 77 and 84)*, or the Aventine *(see page 143)*.

Capitoline/Campidoglio

B: 30, 40, 44, 46, 60, 62, 63, 64, 70, 81, 85, 87, 95, 117, 170, 492, 571, 628, 630, 780, 810, 850

• SNAPSHOT •

Of Rome's seven hills, the Capitoline (*Campidoglio* or *Capitolino*), though the shortest, is the most venerated. The heart of spiritual and political activity since the 6th century BC, it was once the site of the ancient Temple of Jupiter. It continues to be the locus of Rome's municipal administration, with city hall housed in the Palazzo Senatorio on the central square of Piazza del Campidoglio.

The Capitoline is noted for its religious, political, and historical sites. The Palazzo Senatorio, seat of the Roman Senate from the 12th century, sits at the hill's summit—at the Piazza del Campidoglio. The Capitol in Washington, DC, where the U.S. Congress sits, was named after this revered area. Symbolically, the Capitoline represents one of the pillars of Western civilization. The imposing Piazza del Campidoglio and the Senatorial Palace, both designed by Michelangelo, are examples of Renaissance principles of beauty, harmony, and symmetry, and are worth the climb. Walking through the Capitoline is like taking a stroll through Imperial and Renaissance Rome. The area should also be visited at night when the lighting throws magical auras onto the piazza and the surrounding buildings.

PLACES TO SEE
Landmarks:

At the northern foot of Capitoline Hill is **Piazza Venezia**, a large square with what seems like a perpetual traffic jam. On the west side, **Palazzo Venezia (1)** *(Via del Plebiscito 118, 06-69.99.42.84, museopalazzovenezia. beniculturali.it; hours: Tu–Su 8:30AM–7:30PM)*, built in the 15th century by the Venetian Pope Paul II, is one of Rome's first Renaissance buildings. Over the centuries it metamorphosed from papal residence to Venetian Embassy to French property, until ownership finally reverted to the Italian state in 1916. Mussolini made it his center of operations and stood on the central balcony to give his pompous orations. In a show of fascist insecurity, police kept the crowds moving—maybe a godsend for the many who weren't interested in standing still for *Il Duce's* speeches.

Next to **Palazzo Venezia (1)**, in a small square off **Piazza Venezia**, is the church of **San Marco (2)** *(P.za San Marco 48, 06-679.52.05, www.sanmarcoevangelista.it; hours: Su 9AM–1PM, 4PM–8PM, Tu–Sa 8:30AM–12PM, 4PM–6PM, Aug 4PM–8PM)*, founded in 336 by Pope Mark. It was built on the grounds of what legend claims was the house of St. Mark the Evangelist (patron saint of Venice). It was rebuilt in the 5th century and renovated in the 15th century by Venetian Pope Paul II when he had **Palazzo Venezia (1)** built. Its present Baroque style came from an 18th-century reconstruction. There are lions everywhere, from the medieval sculptures at the main entrance to the ceiling decorations. They were the symbol of St. Mark and the Barbo family crest of Pope Paul II. The church houses tombs of various Venetians, but the most notorious gravestone is that of Vanozza Catanei, mother of the infamous Cesare and Lucrezia Borgia, and mistress of Pope Alexander VI (Rodrigo Borgia).

Across from **San Marco (2)**, on the other side of **Piazza Venezia**, is the Victor Emmanuel Monument **Il Vittoriano (3)** *(P.za Venezia, 06-699.17.18, 06-678.06.64; hours: daily 9:30AM–4PM, summer til 5PM)*, a colossal gaudy tribute to Vittorio Emanuele II, the first king of unified Italy. It has been nicknamed "the wedding cake" and "the typewriter" because of its tiers of stark marble slabs and toothlike columns in semicircular formation. A gilt bronze statue of the king astride a horse stands in the middle, atop sculpted marble. The bombastic architecture has led Romans to say that it's the perfect viewing spot in Rome—because it's the only place where you don't see **Il Vittoriano (3)**.

Behind **Il Vittoriano (3)** is the medieval church **Santa Maria in Aracoeli (4)** *(P.za d'Aracoeli, 06-679.81.55, 06-6976.38.39; hours: May–Sep daily 9AM–6:30PM, Oct–Apr daily 9:30AM–5:30PM)*. To reach this 6th-century church of "St. Mary of the Altar in the Sky," you must climb the 14th-century **Aracoeli Stairway (5)**. Some believe it was built in gratitude for the lifting of the plague of the Black Death; with 124 marble steps it might send some to their death of fatigue, the more fit to a euphoric state. When 17th-century backpacking

121

tourists unrolled their sleeping bags on the steps, Prince Caffarelli, a hilltop inhabitant, chased them away by rolling barrels filled with stones down the steps. **Santa Maria in Aracoeli (4)** was built on the site of an ancient temple to Juno and contains works and relics spanning the 3rd century BC to the 15th century AD. The interior of the church is imposing, with 22 columns taken from ancient Roman buildings marking the central nave. A Cosmatesque floor and works (some signed) by major artists of the 13th, 14th, and 15th centuries grace the church. Relics of St. Helena, mother of 4th-century Emperor Constantine, are also located here.

Go back down the **Aracoeli Stairway (5)** (note the **Roman Insula**, ruins of a tenement building of Imperial Rome,

at the foot of the stairway on the Via del Teatro di Marcello) and up the adjoining **Cordonata (6)** *(from Via del Teatro di Marcello)*. This magnificent sweeping staircase leads up to the fabulous **Piazza del Campidoglio (7)**. Take time to relish Michelangelo's gorgeous geometrical designs on the pavement of the piazza and the graceful beauty of the surrounding buildings. In the center of the piazza is a copy of a majestic statue of Marcus Aurelius on a horse (the original is in the Palazzo Nuovo). Facing the **Cordonata (6)** is the **Palazzo Senatorio (8)**, now the offices of the mayor of Rome.

The two other stunning buildings of the **Piazza del Campidoglio (7)** are the **Capitoline Museums (9)** *(see below)*, **Palazzo Nuovo** and **Palazzo dei Conservatori**, with collections of some of the finest specimens of art from ancient Rome up through the Renaissance and Baroque eras. Michelangelo designed the **Cordonata (6)**, the **Piazza del Campidoglio (7)**, and the façades of its palazzi (**Senatorio (8)**, **Nuovo**, and **Conservatori**), though all were completed long after his death. The **Tabularium** joins the two Capitoline Museums. It was the ancient Roman archive, the building on which the **Palazzo Senatorio (8)** was built. Dating from 78 BC, the **Tabularium** affords a spectacular view over the Roman Forum, especially resplendent at sunset.

The **Temple of Jupiter (10)** *(Via del Tempio di Giove)*, built around 509 BC, stood at the southern apex of Capitoline Hill. Today, only ruins remain of the Grecian-style rectangular temple and its Roman podium; from those ruins archaeologists surmise the structure to have been about as big as the Pantheon. At the southern end of the temple ruins is the **Tarpeian Rock (11)** *(Via del Tempio di Giove and Via di Monte Caprino)*, *Rupe Tarpea*, the cliff from which traitors to ancient Rome were flung to their death.

Arts & Entertainment:
The ★**CAPITOLINE MUSEUMS (9)** *(P.za del Campidoglio 1, 06-06.08, www.musei capitolini.org; hours: Tu–Su 9AM–8PM)*, **Palazzo Nuovo** and **Palazzo dei Conservatori**, house bronze sculptures from the 5th century BC

TOP PICK!

through the 4th century AD, Classical sculptures, and paintings by Renaissance and Baroque masters. The collection was started in 1471 when Pope Sixtus IV gave several bronze sculptures to the city. In 1566 Pope Pius V added to the holdings. By 1734 the accumulation was significant, and Pope Clement XII turned the **Palazzo Nuovo** into the first public museum in the world.

Gathered in the **Palazzo Nuovo** is one of Europe's most important collections of ancient sculpture. Many of these pieces took inspiration from or were direct copies of Greek statues. Among its many masterpieces, the museum houses the 2nd-century bronze statue of Marcus Aurelius which once stood in the center of Piazza del Campidoglio (7) (a copy has taken its place there); statues of drunken old men and women; the *Red Faun* (a marble satyr and the basis for Nathaniel Hawthorne's novel *The Marble Faun*); busts of emperors, philosophers, and poets; the *Dying Gaul*; and the flirtatious 1st-century BC *Capitoline Venus*. The latter was based on the Greek *Cnidian Aphrodite*, a marble figure on the island of Kos so erotic that purportedly, a 4th-century BC local who embraced the goddess was caught literally with his pants down.

Once the city tribunal during the Middle Ages, the **Palazzo dei Conservatori** contains a collection of sculpture ranging from 1st-century BC bronze statues to Renaissance and Baroque marble sculptures. The famous *Spinario*, a 1st-century BC bronze of a boy taking out a splinter from his foot, is there. Also in the collection is the renowned 5th-century BC Etruscan bronze of the She-Wolf suckling Romulus and Remus (the twin babies, founders of Rome, were added in the 15th century). In the museum's courtyard are the marble head and other fragments of a huge 4th-century statue of Emperor Constantine I, taken from the Basilica of Constantine and Maxentius in the Roman Forum *(see page 131)*. The museum also houses paintings by great masters such as Veronese, Tintoretto, Rubens, Caravaggio, and Titian, among others.

The **Museum of Palazzo Venezia (12)** *(Via del Plebiscito 118, 06-69.99.41, 06-69.99.43.88, museopalazzo venezia.beniculturali.it; hours: Tu–Su 8:30AM–7:30PM)* houses a fine collection of paintings from the Renaissance through the 18th century, tapestries from around Europe, bronzes, silver, majolica, Neapolitan figurines in ceramic, and Baroque sculptures in terra cotta. In the eastern wing of the palazzo, where special exhibitions are held, you can see Mussolini's office, the *Sala del Mappamondo*, named for the 16th-century map of the world that hung there.

PLACES TO EAT & DRINK
Where to Eat:
Caffè Capitolino (13) (€) *(P.za Caffarelli 4, 06-69.19.05.64; hours: Tu–Su 9AM–8PM)* is a café on the terrace of Palazzo Caffarelli, with a spectacular view of Rome. It offers finger sandwiches, pastries, ice cream, and beverages, and is a great place to rest after all the hill climbing. The café isn't marked, so from the top of the Cordonata stairway, turn right and follow the incline.

FORUM & COLOSSEUM

B: 81, 85, 87, 117, 175, 186, 810, 850
M: B to Colosseo

• SNAPSHOT •

TOP PICK!

Adjacent to the Campidoglio is the *Foro Romano*, the ★**ROMAN FORUM**. It is on these stones that ancient republicans, emperors, philosophers, patricians, and plebeians met to discuss and debate the political, social, and judicial matters of the day. At the far eastern end of the Forum, Emperor Vespasian built the Colosseum. The stadium is amazingly well preserved, but an eeriness pervades the arena and its underground animal cages, reminding the spectator of its gory past.

Like a mass of jigsaw puzzle pieces, the Forum is a conglomeration of ruins, majestic columns, partitions, and walls, with the towering Colosseum rising in the background. All these vestiges of an ancient civilization spark

the imagination, allowing history and dreams to commingle. Here, in the Forum, was the heartbeat of the people of the Republic. Today, on that same soil in 21st-century Rome, modern humanity encounters ancient ghosts. It is an encounter you won't want to miss.

Entrances and tickets:

Via dei Fori Imperiali, Largo Romolo e Remo, Via del Foro Romano, and by the Arch of Titus (on Via Sacra), 06-39.96.77.00/06-06.08; hours: daily 8:30AM–1 hour before sunset, unless otherwise specified.

Entrance to the Roman Forum and the *Imperial Fora* is free. You must pay a fee to enter the Colosseum. Combination tickets with other site locations are available. Visit or call for tickets: *Via di San Gregorio 30 and near the Arch of Titus on Via Sacra (Roman Forum), 06-39.96.77.00.*

The Visitors' Center provides guided tours: *Via dei Fori Imperiali, 06-06.08; hours: Apr–Sept daily 8:30AM–7:15PM, Oct–Mar daily 8:30AM–4:30PM.*

Mobile refreshment carts offer drinks and snacks. For restaurants, bars, and shops, go to the nearby Monti area *(see Chapter 3, page 84)* or the Celio *(see Chapter 4, page 102)*. Cafés and restaurants abound on nearby Via Cavour.

PLACES TO SEE
Landmarks:

In constructing Via dei Fori Imperiali, Mussolini bulldozed through ancient ruins and medieval and Renaissance buildings constructed on top of them. The street was made to connect his headquarters in Palazzo Venezia to the Colosseum. The avenue more or less separates the area of the *fora* into the **Roman Forum** to the south and the **Imperial Fora**, with some exceptions, to the north.

In the northern sector, individual emperors built administrative centers that doubled as monuments to themselves. The remains of the last of these, the 2nd-century **Forum of Trajan**, cover the northeastern part of this area. At what would have been the north end of the forum is **Trajan's Column (14)** *(Via dei Fori Imperiali)*, wonderfully sculpted and incredibly well preserved.

East of the column are **Trajan's Markets (15)** *(Via IV Novembre 94, 06-679.00.48/06-06.08; hours: Tu–Su 9AM–7PM)*, an early 2nd-century shopping mall. Shops sold silks, jewelry, spices, flowers, fruit, and fish, among other products, and offices in the building rationed free corn to hungry citizens.

On the other side of Via dei Fori Imperiali is the first of the *Imperial Fora*—the **Forum of Julius Caesar (16)**

128

(Via del Carcere Tulliano, 06-39.96.77.00). Caesar claimed that he was descended from Venus, the goddess of love, and he built a temple in his forum dedicated to Venus Genetrix. In it were statues of Venus, Caesar, and Cleopatra.

Southwest of Caesar's Forum, at the foot of the Capitoline, is the **Mamertine Prison (17)** *(Clivio Argentario 1, 06-698.961, 800-917.430; hours: daily 9AM–5PM, summer til 7PM)*—two underground dungeons, one beneath the other, where inmates were chained and left to die or executed in a lower cell.

Southeast of Caesar's and Trajan's *fora* is the **Forum of Augustus (18)** *(P.za del Grillo 1)*, opened in 2 BC to commemorate Augustus's victory over Caesar's assassins, Brutus and Cassius, in the Battle of Philippi (42 BC). Four Corinthian columns demarcate the area where the Temple of Mars the Avenger stood—with a statue of Mars suspiciously resembling Augustus himself. Walking through Augustus's shrine to himself, you reach the **Forum of Nerva (19)** *(P.za del Grillo 1, by way of Forum of Augustus)*. Much of it was bulldozed, along with Renaissance shops and bars built on top of it, when Mussolini built the Via dei Fori Imperiali.

In the western half of the **Roman Forum**, toward Capitoline Hill, the most spectacular and well-preserved structure is the **Arch of Septimius Severus (20)**, built in AD 203 for the tenth anniversary of Emperor Septimius Severus's rule.

The **Curia (21)** was the Roman Senate, a building destroyed several times by fire and rebuilt by Julius Caesar (52 BC), then Domitian (AD 94), and again by Diocletian (3rd century AD). Diocletian's **Curia** was restored in 1937 and is the structure existing today. The original 3rd-century floor remains, as do the speaker's platform and the risers where the 300 senators sat in council.

On the other side of the **Arch of Septimius Severus (20)** are the ruins of the **Temple of Saturn (22)**, a platform and eight enormous columns with part of the entablature above them. According to myth, the god Saturn presided over an era of peace and prosperity free from war, crime, slavery, and private property. The three nearby columns are what's left of the **Temple of Vespasian**. On the other side of the **Temple of Saturn (22)** are the ruins of the imperial **Rostra (23)**, the platform from which speeches were made to the citizens of Rome. The most famous was Mark Antony's oration after Julius Caesar was assassinated in 44 BC: "Friends, Romans, Countrymen, lend me your ears. . . ."

Off to the side of the **Temple of Saturn (22)** is a large area of stones, the remains of **Basilica Julia (24)**. In ancient Rome, basilicas were law courts and places where state fiscal matters were negotiated. Civil law cases were tried in **Basilica Julia (24)**, where 180 magistrates presided in four courtrooms. Lawyers paid people to come cheer them and boo their opponents. At the end of **Basilica**

Julia (24) is the Temple of Castor and Pollux (25), first built in 484 BC to honor the mythical twins. They appeared during the Battle of Lake Regillus, helping the Romans vanquish the Tarquin kings, then showed themselves again in the Forum—on the spot where the temple was then built. Three beautiful Corinthian columns dating from AD 6, reconstructed numerous times after fires, remain.

The eastern half of the **Roman Forum** picks up at this point. Several notable ruins are located in this part of the **Via Sacra** ("Sacred Way"), the main street of the Forum and the route taken by triumphal and religious processions from the Arch of Titus (26) *(see page 132)* to Capitoline Hill. On the north side of the **Via Sacra** is perhaps the most bizarre sight of the entire area. The Temple of Antonius and Faustina (27), with its ancient steps, columns, and front porch, is attached to the Baroque façade of the church of San Lorenzo in Miranda, making it appear as though the 2nd-century temple is capped by a Baroque hat, with the church caged by the old temple columns. The circular structure next door with a cupola on top is the Temple of Romulus (28), dating from the 4th century and built for the son of Emperor Maxentius.

Continuing along the **Via Sacra**, you come to the substantial remains of the Basilica of Constantine and Maxentius (29), the largest structure in the Forum. This 4th-century building was begun by Maxentius, emperor of the Western part of then-split Rome, and completed by Constantine. After Constantine conquered Maxentius in battle in AD 312, he became ruler of the entire Western Roman Empire. Three enormous coffered barrel vaults give a sense of the immensity of the original building.

Across the **Via Sacra** to the south, and past a middle area of ruins, are the remains of the **Temple of Vesta (30)** and of the **House of the Vestal Virgins (31)**. The Temple was dedicated to Vesta, goddess of the hearth, and her cult of the Vestals, six virgins charged with keeping the sacred flame of Vesta continuously lit. The Vestals, the only female priests in Rome, came from noble families, had to be virgins, and were granted privileges that no other women in Rome had. As soon as they were chosen for service, the girls were taken to live in the **House of the Vestal Virgins (31)** with the other priestesses. A large three-story building with around 50 rooms, the house had a central courtyard with a lily pond and goldfish. To the east of the Vestals' ruins is the **Arch of Titus (26)**, a triumphal monument built in AD 81 to commemorate Vespasian and his son Titus's sacking of Jerusalem.

Directly north of the arch is the **Antiquarium Forense (32)**, a small archaeological museum *(see page 134)*. It is housed within the church **Santa Francesca Romana (33)**, where a flagstone is marked with the supposed knee prints of Saints Peter and Paul. Just beyond the Forum to the east is the **Arch of Constantine (34)** *(between Via San Gregorio and P.za del Colosseo)*, a monument to Constantine's victory over Maxentius.

Constantine's arch stands beside one of Rome's most famous and emblematic structures, the ★COLOSSEUM (35) *(P.za del Colosseo, 06-39.96.77.00, 06-06.08; hours: daily 8:30AM–sunset)*. When Nero committed suicide in AD 68, his outrageously opulent house, **Domus Aurea** *(see page 86)*, where he held orgies and decadent garden parties, was demolished. The lake was drained, and in its place Emperor Vespasian built the Colosseum (35). The majestic amphitheatre seated at least 55,000 (some say 87,000) people, who entered and exited through 80 arched entrances. Internal corridors allowed rapid access to the seating areas. This architectural plan has formed the basis for amphitheaters and sports arenas to this day.

Blood sport was the hallmark of the Colosseum (35), with the combatants any combination of professionally trained gladiators (who were slaves, condemned criminals, and prisoners of war), untrained unfortunates, and wild animals fighting one another to the death. While entry to the gory shows was free, the spectators were separated by social class and sex. The central box with front-row seats was reserved for the emperor and senators; priests and magistrates had the next tier up, and above them were foreign diplomats. Women were relegated to the top floor, except for the Vestal Virgins, who had front-row seating alongside the emperor. Wild animal fights were finally abolished in AD 523.

Arts & Entertainment:

Antiquarium Forense (32), the Archaeological Museum of the Forum, located within the convent of **Santa Francesca Romana (33)**, contains pieces excavated from the Forum. Iron Age funerary urns, skeletons, and fragments of statues and architectural details from buildings in the Forum are part of the collection.

PLACES TO EAT & DRINK
Where to Eat:

Typical Roman dishes are served at the pleasant outdoor tables of **Ristorante Mario's (36)** (€-€€) *(P.za del Grillo 9, 06-679.37.25, www.ristorantemarios.com; hours: Tu–Su 12PM–3:30PM, 6:30PM–11PM)*. Nearby in the Monti area *(see page 84)* are more restaurants.

WHERE TO STAY

A couple of hotels in the Forum area are worth considering. The **Fori Imperiali Cavalieri (37)** (€-€€) *(Via Frangipane 34, 06-679.62.46, www.hotelforiimperiali cavalieri.com)* is quiet with excellent service and good value for the style and comfort it offers. The hotel has been renovated and includes dataports in the rooms. **Hotel Forum (38)** (€€-€€€) *(Via Tor de' Conti 25-30, 06-679.24.46, www.hotelforumrome.com)*, a converted convent, is warm and pleasant, with walnut paneling and a roof-garden restaurant with a view of the **Imperial Fora**.

Also check out hotels in the nearby Monti area *(see page 89)*, the Celio *(see page 108)*, or the Aventine *(see page 149)*.

PALATINE

B: 60, 75, 85, 87, 117, 175, 271, 571, 673, 810, 850
M: B to Circo Massimo or Colosseo

● SNAPSHOT ●

In ancient times, the affluent and powerful made their homes on the hills, whose elevation and distance from the swampy valleys in between made them desirable. Of these, the Palatine was the most exclusive residential location. It was close enough to the business and political center of the Forum but far enough away to be quiet and pleasant. The first emperor, Augustus, was born there and lived in a modest home. Emperors Tiberius, Caligula, and Domitian built palatial homes on the hill. Nero's *Domus Aurea*, centered on the Esquiline and Celio Hill, encompassed an area reaching as far as the Palatine, with his large lake in the valley between them (in what is now the Colosseum). But well before Imperial Rome (27 BC to AD 476), before even the Republic (509 BC to 27 BC), Romulus founded Rome on the Palatine in 753 BC. According to the famous legend, the twins Romulus and Remus were raised by a she-wolf in a cave on Palatine Hill. Archaeologists believe that Iron Age huts (dating from the 9th to 7th centuries BC) on the Palatine were the first settlements of Rome.

ENTRANCE AND TICKETS:
You must pay a fee to enter the Palatine. Combination tickets with other site locations are available. Visit or call for tickets: *Via di San Gregorio 30* and near the Arch of Titus on *Via Sacra (Roman Forum), 06-39.96.77.00/06-06.08. Hours: daily 8:30AM–sunset.*

For restaurants, bars, shops, and hotels, go to the nearby areas of the Celio *(see page 102)* or the Aventine *(see page 143)* or slightly further, to the Monti district *(see page 84).*

PLACES TO SEE
Landmarks:

From the **Roman Forum**, you can enter the Palatine at the **Farnese Gardens (39)**. It was built in the 16th century by Cardinal Alessandro Farnese on the ruins of the *Domus Tiberius* (*domus* means "house," and the houses of most of the emperors here were palaces). The wonderful 17th-century pavilion at the top of the hill has fabulous views of the Forum. Behind this pavilion, along the garden's southeastern border is the **Cryptoporticus (40)**, an underground tunnel that was part of a network connecting Nero's *Domus Aurea* in the Esquiline to Palatine Hill. Stucco reliefs ornament the vaults, and slits allow light to filter in.

One of the better-preserved buildings on the Palatine is near the southern tip of the **Farnese Gardens (39)**. The **House of Livia (41)** is where Emperor Augustus lived with Livia, his second wife. Faded frescoes give a sense of the decoration of this imperial domicile, and though it was more modest than that of later emperors, it has lasted longer. Some of the frescoes depict mythological scenes; others are *trompe-l'oeil* paintings.

Near Livia's house are the ruins of the **Temple of Cybele (42)**, a mother-figure goddess sacred to a 2nd-century BC cult. The cult's priests castrated themselves in wild ritual sacrifices to the goddess, who reigned over the fertility of nature. All that remains of the temple is rubble, a

platform, and a decapitated statue of Cybele. Nearby are the remnants of three huts dating from the 9th century BC—the **Huts of Romulus (43)**. Romulus, Rome's legendary founder, killed his twin Remus and established the city here.

In AD 81 Emperor Domitian of the Flavian dynasty built a palace that was to be the imperial residence for the next 300 years. It had two sections. **Domus Flavia (44)** was the official palace, while **Domus Augustana (45)** was the private home. A courtyard, fountains, and dining room were at the entrance of **Domus Flavia (44)**. The name of the **Domus Augustana (45)**, Domitian's private home, derives from the Latin *augustus*, which means "favored by the gods." Domitian may have been august, but he was also paranoid. Terrified of being murdered, he had his courtyard walls lined with shiny stones to act as mirrors in which he could spy an intruder. This didn't prevent him from being assassinated in his bedroom; one theory is that his wife was behind it.

An oblong **Stadium (46)** to the east of the **Domus Augustana (45)** was part of the palace. Its use is unknown; it may have been a racetrack or garden. In the 6th century it was used for footraces. The wall fragments and arches to the south are part of the **Domus Septimius Severus (47)**, a 2nd-century AD extension of the imperial palace.

Arts & Entertainment:
The Palatine Museum (48), tucked between the Domus Flavia (44) and the Domus Augustana (45), is an *antiquarium* of objects and pieces of buildings from the Palatine. These include artifacts and human remains from the 8th-century BC hilltop settlements, as well as models of the huts, and statues, busts, and eave decorations. Parts of the foundation of Domitian's palace are evident in the museum's structure.

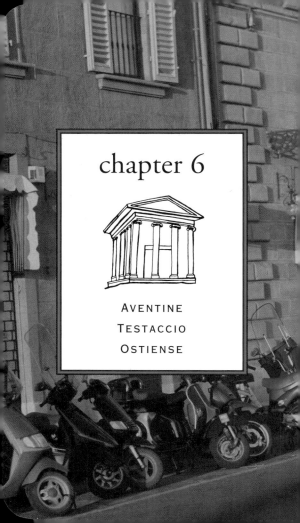

chapter 6

AVENTINE
TESTACCIO
OSTIENSE

AVENTINE TESTACCIO OSTIENSE

Places to See:
1. San Teodoro
2. Santa Maria della Consolazione
3. Casa dei Crescenzi
4. Temple of Portunus
5. Temple of Hercules Victor
6. Santa Maria in Cosmedin
7. Circo Massimo
8. Roseto di Roma
9. Parco Savello
10. Santa Sabina
11. Piazza dei Cavalieri di Malta
12. Sant'Anselmo
29. Monte Testaccio
30. Protestant Cemetery
31. Pyramid of Caius Cestius
32. MACRO Testaccio
33. Villaggio Globale
34. Teatro di Documenti
50. Centrale Montemartini
56. San Paolo Fuori Le Mura

Places to Eat & Drink:
13. Trattoria San Teodoro
14. Apuleius
15. Ristorante Consolini
16. Osteria del Campidoglio
17. Alvaro al Circo Massimo
18. Clamur
19. Shangò
35. Volpetti Più
36. Né Arte Né Parte
37. Pecorino
38. Agustarello
39. Checchino dal 1887
40. Joia
41. Divinare
42. Caruso Café de Oriente
43. Caffè Latino
44. Alibi
51. Planet Roma
52. Ex-Magazzini
53. Goa Club
54. Nazca

Where to Shop:
20. Longobardi
21. Il Negozio Benedettino della Badia Primaziale di Sant'Anselmo
45. Testaccio Market
46. Volpetti
47. Le Bambole
48. Boccanera

Where to Stay:
22. Kolbe Hotel Rome
23. Forty Seven
24. Residence Palazzo al Velabro
25. Hotel Aventino
26. Hotel San Anselmo
27. Hotel Villa San Pio
28. Hotel Domus Aventina
49. Santa Prisca
55. Hotel Abitart

Rome is the city of echoes, the city of illusions, and the city of yearning.

—*Giotto di Bondone*

AVENTINE

B: P.za Bocca della Verità—23, 44, 63, 81, 95, 160, 170, 280, 628, 715, 716, 780, 781; Santa Sabina—23, 280, 716

M: B to Circo Massimo or Piramide

● SNAPSHOT ●

Some 2,000 years ago the area along the Tiber River in the Aventine stirred with commerce and river transportation. The ports gave the area a rough quality, and sailors and merchants took up quarters there. In the triangle between the northern foot of Aventine Hill and Capitoline Hill, in the area around what is now Piazza Bocca della Verità, the outdoor markets of Forum Boarium (cattle) and Forum Holitorium (vegetables) were frequented by plebeians.

The plebeians, the lowest class of Roman citizens, were made up of peasants, traders, builders, and other manual laborers. As the merchants on Aventine Hill became more affluent, they constructed their own homes, and the area began to undergo gentrification. By 27 BC, the beginning of the Empire, the Aventine had become upscale; by the 5th century it was dotted with luxury palazzi. Today, the Aventine is an exclusive residential neighborhood, full of expensive villas with luxurious gardens and swimming pools. Quiet, tree-lined, and relatively secluded, Aventine Hill nevertheless encompasses a number of noteworthy landmarks and one of Rome's loveliest green spots, Parco Savello.

PLACES TO SEE
Landmarks:

One of Rome's little gems is **San Teodoro (1)** *(Via di San Teodoro 7, 06-678.66.24; hours: daily 9AM–12:30PM)*, a 6th-century church snuggled into the foot of Palatine Hill in the triangle along the river formed by the Aventine, Capitoline, and Palatine. The small round exterior, built on the ruins of an ancient granary, is intriguing, while the splendid interior is marked by its 6th-century mosaics and 15th-century Florentine cupola. Not far away, beneath the cliff of the **Tarpeian Rock** *(see page 123)*, where criminals and traitors were dropped to their deaths, stands **Santa Maria della Consolazione (2)** *(P.za della Consolazione 84, 06-678.46.54; hours: daily 6:30AM–12PM, 3:30PM–6PM)*. It was named after an image of the Virgin Mary that 14th-century nobleman Giordanello degli Alberini, a condemned man himself, had placed there to console the unfortunates as they plunged over the cliff. That icon is located in the church's presbytery.

In the area along the riverfront are numerous structures, in various states of preservation, that are reminders of the busy cattle market that once energized the docks in this district. Fragments of ancient Roman buildings are still embedded in the ruins of the 11th-century **Casa dei Crescenzi (3)** *(Via Luigi Petroselli)*, a fortress built by the Crescenzi family to control the docks and collect tolls from the Ponte Rotto. For more divine protection, the two 2nd-century BC temples of the Forum Boarium are in excellent shape because they were turned into Christian churches during the Middle Ages. The **Temple of Portunus (4)** (*P.za Bocca della Verità*), dedicated to the god of rivers and ports but once called the Temple of *Fortuna Virilis*, or "Men's Fortunes," is a rectangular structure with columns on the front porch. Behind it is the other shrine, small and circular: the **Temple of Hercules Victor (5)** (*P.za Bocca della Verità*). It was dedicated to the he-man who killed a giant for stealing his cattle. Because this small circular shrine resembles the Temple of Vesta in the Roman Forum, it has also been called by that name.

The beautiful 6th-century **Santa Maria in Cosmedin (6)** (*P.za Bocca della Verità 18, 06-678.14.19, 06-678.7759; hours: Apr–Sept daily 9:30AM–6PM, Oct–Mar daily 9:30AM–5PM*) has an amusing mix of medieval and Romanesque designs, with a 12th-century bell tower and exquisite mosaics inside. The church is most famous for the large stone mask embedded in the portico wall. The face of a man with wild hair, full beard, and mouth agape, the **Bocca della Verità**, or "Mouth of Truth," is the legendary test of lying criminals and cheating spouses. A liar who put his/her hand in the mouth, the legend has it, would end up without a hand—the stone jaws would clamp down and cut it off!

Off to the southeast of the Mouth of Truth, and below the Palatine, stretches the ancient Roman chariot-racing arena, the **Circo Massimo (7)** *(Via del Circo Massimo)*, in use from the 4th century BC until AD 549. Now just a grassy expanse, the stadium once held 300,000 spectators. The Aventine is home to several beautiful parks. Southwest of the **Circo Massimo (7)**, off the Piazzale Ugo la Malfa, is the **Roseto di Roma (8)** *(Clivio dei Pubblici)*, at the foot of the hill. This park, once the 17th-century site of a Jewish cemetery, was turned into a rose garden in the 1950s, with avenues placed to form the shape of a menorah.

To the west, atop Aventine Hill, **Parco Savello (9)** *(P.za Pietro d'Illiria)*, officially **Il Giardino degli Aranci**, or "Garden of the Orange Trees," is one of Rome's gems. It has a fabulous view stretching from Gianicolo Hill and St. Peter's Basilica across the river to **Il Vittoriano** in Piazza Venezia. Located within the walls of the Savelli family fortress, the park is full of orange trees, commemorating St. Dominic, who first brought orange trees to Italy from Spain in 1220. The original tree supposedly still thrives in the garden of **Santa Sabina (10)** *(P.za Pietro d'Illiria 1, 06-57.94.06.00/06-579.401; hours: daily 8:15AM–12:30PM, 3:30PM–6PM)*, an early Christian basilica. Built in the 5th century on what was once the home of a martyred Roman woman named Sabina, the

146

magnificent interior is arcaded along the nave with 24 Corinthian columns.

The beautiful walled **Piazza dei Cavalieri di Malta (11)** was designed by Piranesi in the 18th century, with cypress trees, obelisks, and military trophies adding to its ornate allure. If you see people peeping through the keyhole of the **Priory of the Knights of Malta** (at No. 3), don't be appalled—they're looking at the famous keyhole view of the dome of St. Peter's Basilica across the river in the Vatican.

Arts & Entertainment:
Free concerts and church music are common in Rome's hundreds of churches, but few have what is offered at the Aventine. On Sundays (October–July) at 9AM mass and 7:15PM vespers, the Benedictine church of **Sant'Anselmo (12)** *(P.za Cavalieri di Malta 5, 06-579.11, www.santanselmo.net)* echoes with Gregorian chants.

PLACES TO EAT & DRINK
Where to Eat:
Chic, inviting, and upscale, **Trattoria San Teodoro (13) (€€€)** *(Via dei Fienili 49-51, 06-678.09.33, www.st-teodoro.it; hours: daily 12:50PM–3:30PM, 7:50PM–11PM, closed Su Nov–Mar)* is known for its sophisticated cuisine—especially the seafood. The setting, on a quiet medieval street, is beautiful—especially the romantic patio outside.

With an original portion of an ancient Temple of Diana preserved within its interior, *ristorante* **Apuleius (14)** (€€-€€€) *(Via del Tempio di Diana 15, 06-57.28.92.29, www.apuleius.it; hours: lunch: 12:30PM–2PM, dinner 8PM–11PM, no Sa lunch, closed Su)* is a unique, romantic place to dine. Enjoy traditional Italian fare al fresco at multilevel **Ristorante Consolini (15)** (€-€€) *(Via Marmorata 28, 06-57.30-01.48, www.ristoranteconsolini.it; call for hours, book ahead)*, situated at the foot of Mount Aventine. At **Osteria del Campidoglio (16)** (€) *(Via dei Fienili 56, 06-678.02.50; call for hours)*, you can count on good Roman favorites, such as hot dishes like *bucatini all'amatriciana*. Tables outside have a view of Santa Maria della Consolazione (2). The reasonable prices at **Alvaro al Circo Massimo (17)** (€-€€) *(Via dei Cerchi 53, 06-678.61.12; hours: Tu–Sa 12:30PM–2:30PM, 7PM–11PM, Su 12:30PM–2:30PM)* make this laid-back seafood restaurant a good deal. Try the linguini with lobster sauce, risotto with truffles, or grilled porcini mushrooms.

Bars & Nightlife:

Clamur (18) *(P.za dell'Emporio 2, 06-575.45.32; hours: Su–Th 7PM–12AM, F–Sa 7PM–1:30AM)* is an English pub with Italian flair. Ales and lagers abound. Shake things up a bit at discoteca **Shangò (19)** *(Via di San Saba 11, 0347-116.75.81, www.romaexclusiveparty.com/discoteche/roma/discoteca-shango-roma/; hours: F & Sa 11:30PM–4:30AM, evening dress required, pairs & mixed groups 23 & over)*. For more nightlife, check out Testaccio and Ostiense *(see pages 151 and 157)*, or Monti *(see page 84)*.

WHERE TO SHOP

At **Longobardi (20)** *(Via dei Fienili 43/A, 06-678.11.04)*, the wares are silver and gold, from jewelry to tableware, all made in Italy. In a cute cottage beside the Benedictine abbey of **Sant'Anselmo (12)**, **Il Negozio Benedettino della Badia Primaziale di Sant'Anselmo (21)** *(P.za dei Cavalieri di Malta 5, 06-579.11; hours: Tu–Su 10AM–12PM, 4PM–7PM)* sells things made in monasteries worldwide. Beer, soaps, jams, tomato sauces, and fruit juices are among the specialties. But its forte is cosmetics, with creams made from natural products and miraculous potions for various ailments. Be sure to try the abbey's own chocolates, too.

WHERE TO STAY

Great location and fantastic views (the **Roman Forum**) are the draws at **Kolbe Hotel Rome (22)** (€€–€€€) *(Via di San Teodoro 44, 06-679.88.66, www.kolbehotelrome.com)*; this luxury hotel features a spectacular garden. Opposite the Temple of Hercules Victor, **Forty Seven (23)** (€€-€€€) *(Via Petroselli 47, 06-678.78.16, www.fortysevenhotel.com)* is a modern temple of repose. The stern exterior belies a light-filled interior with rooms accented by natural wood and marble bathrooms. Modern amenities include Wi-Fi Internet and a fitness center. Well-appointed suites with kitchenettes make **Residence Palazzo al Velabro (24)** (€–€€€) *(Via del Velabro 16, 06-679.27.58, www.velabro.it)* like a home away from home. Quiet and serene, it's a good choice for a longer stay.

The three Aventino San Anselmo hotels *(06-57.00.57, www.aventinohotels.com)* look like Tuscan villas, with a country twist to the elegant Rococo décor. The spacious rooms are as inviting as the lovely gardens surrounded by pine groves. **Hotel Aventino (25) (€-€€)** *(Via San Domenico 10)*; **Hotel San Anselmo (26) (€-€€)** *(P.za San Anselmo 2)*; **Hotel Villa San Pio (27) (€-€€)** *(Via Santa Melania 19)*.

A transformed 14th-century convent with a 17th-century façade, **Hotel Domus Aventina (28) (€-€€)** *(Via di Santa Prisca 11B, 06-574.61.35, www.hoteldomusaventina. com)* is elegant, demure, and serene. Copies of classical artifacts, prints, and murals add to the refined ambience, while the views from the terrace and balconies are beautiful.

TESTACCIO

B: Protestant Cemetery area—23, 60, 75, 118, 271, 715; Monte Testaccio area: 23, 30, 75, 280, 716

M: B to Piramide

• SNAPSHOT •

Testaccio got its name from the huge amount of terra cotta shards *(testae)* that piled up over the centuries in a "mountain" as workers at wine and olive oil warehouses along the river threw out broken clay jugs that stored the goods. A working-class area in the shadow of the bourgeois luxury of the Aventine, Testaccio is one of Rome's hottest nightspots and a magnet for artists, writers, and students seeking an edgier night scene.

What has defined the district since the 19th century is the old slaughterhouse, now being transformed into a cultural center. Though the slaughterhouse closed in 1973, many of its workers still live in the neighborhood. This elderly population gives the area its lively color and diversity. Where soccer teams are concerned, however, there's no diversity whatsoever; the locals are staunch supporters of AS Roma, and the team's red and yellow colors are evident all over the place.

PLACES TO SEE
Landmarks:
Monte Testaccio (29) *(Via Galvani, corner of Via N. Zabaglia 24)* isn't a hill at all; it's a 118-foot rubbish pile of broken terra cotta pots used by ancient traders and shopkeepers to transport and store goods. For some 400 years (from about 140 BC to about AD 250) the shards accumulated into an artificial hill that wasn't recognized for what it is until the late 18th century.

In 1738 the Non-Catholic Cemetery, better known as the **Protestant Cemetery (30)** *(Cimitero Acattolico, Via Caio Cestio 6, 06-574.19.00, cemeteryrome.it; hours: M–Sa 9AM–5PM, Su 9AM–1PM)*, became the burial ground for anyone who wasn't Catholic. Glorious cypresses tower above impressive funerary sculptures, and people from around the world arrive to honor the memories of famous writers, artists, and statesmen, including Goethe, Keats, and Shelley. An afternoon spent here is a reminder of the allure of the Eternal City for which so many foreigners gave up their homelands and to which they left their remains forever. Near the cemetery to the northeast is another burial ground of a wholly monumental variety. The **Pyramid of Caius Cestius (31)** *(Piazzale Ostiense)* is a huge marble pyramid, the tomb of a wealthy and clearly egomaniacal magistrate who died in 12 BC. It was incorporated into the **Aurelian Wall** near the Porta San Paolo.

Arts & Entertainment:

The old *mattatoio*, the slaughterhouse, was for nearly two centuries the defining point of Testaccio, assuring work for its residents. The area is rapidly turning into a "City of the Arts," with plans for museums, multimedia exhibition spaces, the university's architecture department, and a music school. **MACRO Testaccio (32)** *(P.za Orazio Giustiniani 4, 06-06.08/06-671.07.04.00, www.museo macro.org; hours: Tu–Su 4PM–10PM)*, with its two exhibition spaces, is a branch of the **Museum for Contemporary Art of Rome (MACRO)** *(see page 20)* where exhibits of contemporary Italian artists are open until late into the night.

During the winter an old *mattatoio* is also home to the **Villaggio Globale (33)** *(Lungotevere Testaccio 1, entrance Via di Monte Testaccio 22, 0347-413.12.05, www. vglobale.biz; call for hours/shows)*, one of the oldest community centers in Rome. Live concerts, art exhibits, a gay festival, and other events take place in an atmosphere of general joviality in which people mill around with their friends, checking out the wares at commercial stalls and enjoying *panini* and beer from one of the numerous kiosks. In a truly atmospheric setting, the **Teatro di Documenti (34)** *(Via Nicola Zabaglia 42, 06-574.40.34, www.teatrodidocumenti.it; hours: info/ reservations M–F 10:30AM–2:30PM)* presents performances in which the audience moves with the actors up and down in the various wonderful spaces of this 15th-century building.

153

PLACES TO EAT & DRINK
Where to Eat:

The Volpetti brothers, proprietors of the famous deli *(see page 156)*, expanded their food emporium to a cafeteria *(tavola calda)* around the corner from the store. At **Volpetti Più (35) (€)** *(Via Alessandro Volta 8, 06-574.23.52, www.volpetti.com; hours: M–Sa 10:30AM–3:30PM, 5:30PM–9:30PM, Aug M–Sa 10:30AM–3:30PM)* the décor is totally practical but the food is delicious. Lasagnas, salads, pizzas, and other fabulous prepared foods assure the place is always full of customers. At the end of the block, **Né Arte Né Parte (36) (€-€€)** *(Via Luca della Robbia 15-17, 06-575.02.79; hours: Tu–Su 12PM–3PM, 6:30PM–11PM)*, a neighborhood trattoria, offers traditional Italian dishes along with more adventurous creations. Friendly and casual, it is decorated with contemporary art pieces.

The popular **Pecorino (37) (€€)** *(Via Galvani 64, 06-57.25.05.39, www.ristorantepecorino.it; call for hours, closed M)*, with its warm dark wood and modern designs, has lighter versions of the Roman standards. More traditional and working-class, **Agustarello (38) (€-€€)** *(Via Giovanni Branca 98, 06-574.65.85; call for hours)* is a neighborhood standard, serving dishes native to Testaccio: lamb and potatoes, tongue, and *rigatoni alla pajata* (pasta with veal intestines) are true to the meat-packing district's heritage. One of the area's more elegant restaurants, **Checchino dal 1887 (39) (€€-€€€)** *(Via di Monte Testaccio 30, 06-574.38.16, www.checchino-dal-1887.com; hours: Tu–Sa 12:30PM–3PM, 8PM–12AM, closed Aug)* has a mixed menu, including often-over-looked offal (oxtails, hooves, and heads) as well as more refined dishes, such as *agnello alla cacciatora* (lamb with chili peppers and red wine) or *saltimbocca alla romana* (veal with ham and sage), and a great wine list.

Bars & Nightlife:

Joia (40) *(Via Galvani 22, 0347-116.75.81, www.romaexclusiveparty.com/discoteche/roma/discoteca-joia-roma; call for hours)*, a bar-club-restaurant on three floors, carries the ancient Roman theme of decadence and a 17th-century sense of style into its superhip 21st-century surroundings. The wine bar **Divinare (41)** (€) *(Via Aldo Manuzio 12/13, 06-57.25.04.32; hours: M–F 10AM–3PM, 5PM–12AM, Sa 5PM–12AM)* offers an excellent range of cold cuts, *carpaccios*, cheeses, salads, and prepared foods with a large choice of wines. Trendy **Caruso Café de Oriente (42)** *(Via di Monte Testaccio 36, 06-574.50.19, www.carusocafe.com; hours: Tu–Su 11PM–4AM)* is the hip-shaking place for salsa dancing. **Caffè Latino (43)** *(Via di Monte Testaccio 96, 06-578.24.11, 0657.28.85.56, www.caffelatinodiroma.com; hours: W–Sa 10:30PM–3AM, closed June–Sept)* is the granddaddy of the area's disco-bars, with live concerts, acid jazz, and reggae. **Alibi (44)** *(Via di Monte Testaccio 40-44, 06-574.34.48, www.lalibi.it; hours: Oct–May W–Su 11PM–5AM, June–Sept Tu–Su 11PM–5AM)*, Rome's most well-known gay disco, also attracts a mixed crowd. It's another multilevel nightspot with a terrace from which you can check out the human river that enlivens the night.

WHERE TO SHOP

Fresh, cheap produce isn't the only thing for sale at the **Testaccio Market (45)** *(P.za di Testaccio)*; while the produce stalls are a trip, there's also appeal in the high-quality shoes at factory prices. But it's a hit-or-miss shopping experience. Since 1972, the Volpetti brothers have run their gourmet deli with meticulous regard to detail and to the purity of the regional products they sell. You could become addicted to **Volpetti (46)** *(Via Marmorata 47, 06-574.23.52, www.volpetti.com; hours: M–Sa 8AM–2PM, 5PM–8:15PM)*, where cheeses, cold cuts, and specialty products come from all parts of Italy.

Dolls, dolls, and more dolls! **Le Bambole (47)** *(Via Luca della Robbia 11, 06-575.68.95, www.lebambole-testaccio.it)* has the doll market covered, with new, period, and specialty dolls. Saints, madonnas, and Neapolitan crèche pieces are in the offering. It's also a doll hospital, with restorations done by the owner. With all the traipsing up and down hills and in and out of bars, you may feel the urge for a new pair of shoes: check out the footwear at **Boccanera (48)** *(Via Luca della Robbia 36, 06-575.08.47, www.boccanera.it; hours: M 3:30PM–7:30PM, Tu–Su 9:30AM–1:30PM, 3:30PM–7:30PM)*.

WHERE TO STAY

The serene park on the grounds of **Santa Prisca (49) (€)** *(Largo M. Gelsomini 25, 06-574.19.17, www.hotelsantaprisca.it)* and its terraces make up for the dormitory feeling of this converted convent owned by nuns (but not run by them). For more hotel options, check out the Aventine area *(see page 149)*.

OSTIENSE

B: To Montemartini, 23, 716, 769
M: B to Garbatella or Basilica San Paolo

• SNAPSHOT •

Ostiense may lack the charm of Testaccio, but it's breaking out as a trendsetter in clubs, cafés, artists' studios, and shops. The area's old warehouses and power stations have been converted into bars and nightspots. The sight worth visiting during daytime is the Centrale Montemartini, once an electrical power plant, now a fabulous museum. Otherwise, Ostiense is unremarkable by day; rather, the protagonists make their entrance at night.

PLACES TO SEE
Landmarks, Arts & Entertainment:

As Ostiense picks up momentum in its new incarnation as the "in" nightspot, the warehouses and lofts of the district are being converted into artists' studios, bars, and clubs. The 1921 **Centrale Montemartini (50)** *(Via Ostiense 106, 06-06.08, www.centralemontemartini.org; hours: Tu–Su 9AM–7PM)*, Rome's first electric power plant, has been converted into a hip branch of the **Capitoline Museums**. Hellenic statues—gods, goddesses, coy nymphs, leering fauns—mingle with steel tubes, hydraulic pumps, and other machinery of the old generating station in marvelous, provocative coexistence.

PLACES TO EAT & DRINK
Bars & Nightlife:

If you've checked out the hot spots in Testaccio and are aching for more, Ostiense is the next happening area for nightlife. One of the most famous clubs is **Planet Roma (51)** *(Via del Commercio 36, 06-574.78.26, www.planetroma.com; call for hours)*, with three separate areas in a converted warehouse, each featuring different dance-music genres with live concerts, cabarets, and famous DJs. Friday nights are the most wild. Another converted warehouse popular with the trendy crowd is **Ex-Magazzini (52)** *(Via dei Magazzini Generali 8 bis, 06-575.80.40; hours: Tu–Su 9PM–4AM)* (*magazzini* means "warehouses"). The entertainment is diverse: music, film, theater, and naturally the bar. On Sundays there's even an ethnic market on the lower ground floor, with wares from India and Indonesia. Since 1996, **Goa Club (53)** *(Via Giuseppe Libetta 13, 06-574.82.77, www.goaclub.com; call for hours)* has been making its mark as the prime club for electronic music in Rome. Famous musicians and DJs of acid jazz, trip hop, and minimal tech have crossed its threshold, all in a décor that boasts exotic accents of the Raj in India. **Nazca (54)** *(Via del Gazometro 40, 06-45.44.73.72, www.nazcaclub.com; hours: daily 7PM–3AM)* is a popular stop on the club circuit.

WHERE TO STAY

Hotel Abitart (55) (€-€€) *(Via P. Matteucci 10-20, 06-454.31.91, www.abitarthotel.com)* is the only hotel in the Ostiense area. Its eight suites are inspired by different artists, from Picasso to Keith Haring.

OUTSKIRTS OF OSTIENSE

San Paolo Fuori Le Mura (56)
*(Via Ostiense 186, 06-45.43.55.74, 06-541.03.41,
www.abbaziasanpaolo.net; hours: daily 7AM–7PM)
B: 23, 128, 170, 670, 707, 761, 769
M: B to Basilica San Paolo*

In the early 4th century, Emperor Constantine set about legalizing Christianity, building churches in Rome, and spreading the new religion throughout the Empire. He created several basilicas to make the acceptance of Christianity official and to commemorate the martyrdom of important saints. Thus, he built **San Paolo Fuori le Mura** over the tomb of St. Paul, who was martyred some time after AD 62, perhaps in Nero's persecution of Christians. As a Roman citizen, St. Paul could not be crucified; rather, he was executed by decapitation at the nearby **Abbey of the Three Fountains** (named for the three fountains that supposedly gushed up on the spots where Paul's severed head bounced three times). **San Paolo Fuori le Mura** is one of the four major basilicas in Rome, along with St. Peter's, San Giovanni in Laterano, and Santa Maria Maggiore (all but the last were built by Constantine).

chapter 7

TRASTEVERE

GIANICOLO

TRASTEVERE GIANICOLO

Places to See:
1. Ponte Sisto
2. Porta Settimiana
3. Casa della Fornarina
4. Museo di Roma in Trastevere
5. Santa Maria in Trastevere
6. San Crisogono
7. Caserma dei Vigili della VII Coorte
8. Piazza in Piscinula
9. Santa Cecilia in Trastevere
10. San Francesco a Ripa
11. Chiostro dei Genovesi
12. Villa Sciarra
13. San Benedetto in Piscinula
14. Bibli
15. Big Mama
16. Lettere Caffè
17. Teatro Vascello
18. Nuovo Sacher
19. Pasquino
43. Villa Farnesina
44. Palazzo Corsini/Galleria Nazionale d'Arte Antica
45. Orto Botanico
46. Tempietto
47. Fontana dell'Acqua Paola
48. Garibaldi Monument
49. Teatro Ghione
50. Filmstudio
51. Galleria Lorcan O'Neill

Places to Eat & Drink:
20. Checco er Carettiere
21. Doppia Coppia
22. Da Vittorio
23. Il Boom
24. Antico Tevere
25. Big Hilda Café
26. Mr. Brown
27. Café Friends
28. Ombre Rosse Caffè
29. Artù Caffè
30. La Scala
31. RipArte Caffè
32. Il Cortile
52. Scarpone
53. Antico Arco
54. Bar Gianicolo
55. Antica Pesa
56. Terminal Gianicolo

Where to Shop:
33. Joseph Debach
34. Scala Quattordici
35. Almost Corner Bookshop
36. Eredi Baiocco

37. Porta Portese Flea Market
38. Pandora della Malva
39. Officina della Carta

Where to Stay:
38. Residence in Trastevere
39. Hotel Santa Maria
40. La Cisterna
41. Hotel Trastevere
42. Residenza Santa Maria
57. Grand Hotel del Gianicolo
58. Hotel la Rovere

> Rome was a poem pressed into service as a city.
>
> *—Anatole Broyard*

TRASTEVERE

B: Museo di Roma—3, 8, 23, 44, 75, 116, 280, 630, 780; Santa Maria and Santa Cecilia—23, 280, 630, 780; San Francesco—23, 44, 280

• SNAPSHOT •

Trastevere (literally "across the Tiber," or *Tevere*) is a historical quarter that was once agricultural. Farms, vineyards, and gardens served the emperors. Separated as it is by the river from the old historical center and the ancient city, the district has always set itself apart from the rest of Rome. Once a working-class area, its inhabitants pride themselves on their attitude. Sass, pride, independence, toughness, and their own special accent all make *Trasteverini* a breed apart and lend a certain charm to a neighborhood that has retained its picturesque qualities. This aggressive attitude created an "us and them" opposition, with "us," *noantri*, being the *Trasteverini* and "them," *voiatri*, being all other Romans. The quarter's inhabitants celebrate what they see as superiority—reveling in being outsiders—during the *Festa de' Noantri*, a street fair held during the last two weeks of July.

Full of cafés, restaurants, bars, artisans, shops, boutiques, art galleries, and street vendors, it has for many years been a draw for bohemians—intellectuals, artists, filmmakers, and students. Its villagelike character, outsider pride, and hip lifestyle combine to give a slightly gritty edge to an area that, despite gentrification, has retained its authenticity. It is, after all, what the *Trasteverini* believe to be the home of true Romans.

PLACES TO SEE
Landmarks:

The atmospheric 15th-century footbridge **Ponte Sisto (1)** *(at Lungotevere D. Farnesina)* is one of the most beautiful connecting links between Trastevere and the "other" Rome. It was built by Pope Sixtus IV della Rovere, who invested heavily in restoring churches and monuments and commissioning remarkable works of art and buildings, such as the Sistine Chapel and the Hospital of Santo Spirito.

As you step off the pedestrian bridge, you come upon **Piazza Trilussa** with its splendid fountain. The piazza honors the poet Carlo Alberto Salustri, a.k.a. Trilussa, a satiric 19th- and 20th-century poet who wrote in dialect and celebrated the spirit of Rome's everyman. Via Santa Dorotea, on the other side of the square, will bring you to the **Porta Settimiana (2)** *(see page 175)*, just inside of which is **Casa della Fornarina (3)** *(Via di Santa Dorotea 20; closed to the public)*, believed to have been the home of Margherita Luti, a baker's daughter *(fornarina)* and mistress of one of the early 16th century's great masters, Raphael.

The **Museo di Roma in Trastevere (4)** *(see page 167)*, an ethnographic museum of Roman folklore, was once a Carmelite convent attached to the church of Sant' Egidio. The highlight of the area, however, is **Santa Maria in Trastevere (5)** *(P.za Santa Maria in Trastevere, 06-581.48.02; hours: daily 7:30AM–8PM)*, perhaps the first official Christian church in Rome. It was built in the 3rd century by Pope Callixtus I, well before Emperor Constantine legalized Christianity and ended the persecution of followers of the then-minor religion. The church was rebuilt in the 12th century by Pope Innocent II and still maintains its medieval characteristics.

Before Christianity was legalized, the followers of Christ worshipped in private houses, called *tituli*, built expressly for this purpose. Early 12th-century **San Crisogono (6)** *(P.za Sonnino 44, 06-581.82.25; hours: M–Sa 7:30AM–11AM, 4PM–7PM, Su 8AM–1PM, 4PM–7PM)* was built on top of a 5th-century church with 8th-century alterations, which was itself built on one of the oldest *tituli*. Excavations beneath this amazing building can be viewed. The church itself is full of recycled columns, marbles, and mosaics. More excavations—these dating from the 1st century AD—are of the barracks of the ancient Roman fire brigade, the **Caserma dei Vigili della VII Coorte (7)** *(Via della VII Coorte, 06-06.08; open by appt.)*. You can see the courtyard where the firemen rested their weary feet. To rest your own weary feet, make your way over to **Piazza in Piscinula (8)**, beautiful despite all the parked cars.

The southeast sector of Trastevere is dominated by **Santa Cecilia in Trastevere (9)** (*P.za di Santa Cecilia, 06-45.49.27.39, 06-589.92.89, www.benedettinesantacecilia.it; hours: daily 9:15AM–12:45PM, 4PM–6PM, frescoes M–Sa 10AM–12:30PM*). On its grounds stood the home of Cecilia and her husband Valerianus, a patrician whom she converted to Christianity. The Romans attempted to behead her in AD 230, but it took her three days to die. During this time, she sang hymns, thus becoming the patron saint of music. According to legend, the saint's tomb was opened in 1599 and her body was found uncorrupted. Sculptor Stefano Maderno was commissioned to create a likeness of the martyr as she was found; his rendering is displayed at the main altar. The other masterpiece, or fragments of it, located within the church is the 13th-century fresco by Pietro Cavallini, *The Last Judgment*.

Near the Ripa Grande, the port area of Trastevere, was a hospice where St. Francis of Assisi stayed during his 1219 visit to Rome. In the 13th century, **San Francesco a Ripa (10)** (*P.za San Francesco d'Assisi 88, 06-581.90.20; hours: M–Sa 7AM–12PM, 4PM–7PM, Su 7AM–1PM, 4PM–7:30PM*) was built on the site and rebuilt in the 17th century. The cell of St. Francis contains his crucifix and stone pillow as well as his portrait. One of the main highlights of this site is the Bernini sculpture *The Ecstasy of Beata Ludovica Albertoni*, a stunningly sexual rendition of the Franciscan nun's agony and ecstasy.

If Ludovica leaves you breathless, in need of fresh air and serenity, the **Chiostro dei Genovesi (11)** *(Via Anicia 12, bell marked "Sposito," 06-581.24.16, www.confraternita-sgbg.it; hours: Apr–Sept Tu, F 3PM–6PM, Oct–Mar Tu, F 2PM–4PM)* is a fantastic cloister filled with flowers, the first palm tree planted in Rome (1588), and a charming well. You enter the cloister from a wooden door to the right of Santa Maria dell'Orto (the church with the obelisks). Otherwise, head for the palm trees, manicured lawns, rose gardens, and wild grasses of **Villa Sciarra (12)** *(Via Calandrelli 35; Bus: 44, 75; hours: daily 7AM–sunset)* on the outskirts of Trastevere. Jews hid from the Nazis here during World War II. Back at **Piazza in Piscinula (8)**, take in one of Rome's tiniest churches: little **San Benedetto in Piscinula (13)**, *(Piazza in Piscinula 40, 06-58.33.16.09; call for hours, open 9AM Su for Mass)*. "San Benedettino" is said to be located on the site where St. Benedict lived as a boy. Its church bell is the oldest in the city, dating from 1069.

Arts & Entertainment:

Rome's folklore depository, the **Museo di Roma in Trastevere (4)** *(P.za Sant'Egidio 1B, 06-581.65.63, 06-06.08, www.museodiromaintrastevere.it; hours: Tu–Su 10AM–8PM)*, examines the daily life of common people in 18th- and 19th-century Rome. Its more interesting exhibits include wax replicas of places and people in Trastevere. The multilevel bookstore **Bibli (14)** *(Via dei Fienaroli 28, Cultural Center 06-581.45.34, Bookstore 06-588.40.97, www.bibli.it; hours: M 5:30PM–12AM,*

167

Tu–Su 11AM–12AM) hosts readings, films, live music, and talks with film directors and writers. It also has a café and Internet access.

There are other noteworthy artistic venues in Trastevere. Don't miss **Big Mama (15)** *(Vicolo San Francesco a Ripa 18, 06-581.25.51, book ahead, www.bigmama.it; hours: daily 9PM–1:30AM, shows at 10:30PM)* if you love blues and R&B. Well-known acts, both Italian and international, play there. The live music (jazz, folk, rock) at **Lettere Caffè (16)** *(Via San Francesco a Ripa 100-101, 06-97.27.09.91, www.letterecaffe.org; call for hours)* is secondary to its literary readings, poetry slams, and book presentations. For theater and dance performances, catch a show at **Teatro Vascello (17)** *(Via Giacinto Carini 78, 06-588.10.21, www.teatrovascello.it; box office hours: M 9AM–6PM, Tu–F 9AM–9:30PM, Sa 4PM–9:30PM, Su 2:30PM–7:30PM)*, where productions might incorporate video and digital arts into theatrical works.

Independent films and art cinema are the focus of **Nuovo Sacher (18)** *(Largo Aschianghi 1, 06-581.81.16, www.sacherfilm.eu; call for showtimes)*, a movie theater owned by Italian director Nanni Moretti. Here you can catch films not picked up by mainstream distributors. The outdoor cinema is especially pleasant in summer; there's also a bar and bookshop. Another cinema, the three-screen multiplex **Pasquino (19)** *(P.za Sant'Egidio 10, 06-581.52.08; call for showtimes)*, shows films in their original language, mostly mainstream American and English movies.

PLACES TO EAT & DRINK
Where to Eat:

Traditional Roman cuisine doesn't come much better than at **Checco er Carettiere (20)** (€€-€€€) *(Via Benedetta 10, 06-581.70.18, www.checcoercarettiere.it; call for hours)*; pasta *all'amatriciana* is a typical Roman dish. For a great ice cream place, try **Doppia Coppia (21)** (€) *(Via della Scala 51, 06-581.31.74; hours: Apr–Oct M–F 1PM–12AM, Sa–Su 1PM–1AM, Feb, Mar, Nov M–F 1PM–8PM, Sa–Su 1PM–10PM, closed Dec–Jan)*; the Sicilian owners concoct exotic flavors—cinnamon, *amarena*, *cassata*, or coconut—and churn them into the most velvety cream.

Da Vittorio (22) (€) *(Via di San Cosimato 14A, 06-580. 03.53; hours: Tu–Su 12:30PM–3:30PM, 6:45PM–10:30PM)*, on the other hand, is a wonderful neighborhood pizzeria, down to the checked tablecloths and straw-covered wine bottles. The pizzas make the establishment's soccer obsession clear: *Pizza Maradona* is named after the famous Argentinian soccer player while *Pizza Mondiale* gives a nod to the World Soccer Championship. The theme at **Il Boom (23)** (€€-€€) *(Via dei Fienaroli 30a, 06-589.71.96; hours: M–Sa 12PM–3PM, 6PM–late, Su brunch)* is the 1960s, from the photos of Rome to the jukebox selections; the menu is southern Italian. Near the Porta Portese and its famous flea market *(see page 172)*, **Antico Tevere (24)** (€-€€) *(Via Portuense 45,*

06-581.60.54, *www.anticotevere.it*; hours: M–Sa 1PM–3:30PM, 8:30PM–11:30PM) serves Mediterranean-style seafood on a delightful terrace facing the Tiber. Try the *orecchiette alle vongole e zucchini*, octopus *bella vista*, or their fresh *strozzapreti* pasta.

Bars & Nightlife:

Get down and dirty with the rock 'n' roll and cheap drinks at **Big Hilda Café (25)** (Vicolo dei Cinque 33-4, 06-580.33.03; hours: M–Sa 6:30PM–2AM, Su 12PM–2AM). Rub elbows with English ex-pats at **Mr. Brown (26)** (Vicolo dei Cinque 29, 06-581.29.13; hours: daily 7PM–2AM), a sports pub with a musty British décor. Italians have a wonderful *aperitivo* tradition, and at **Café Friends (27)** (P.za Trilussa 34, 06-581.61.11, www.cafe friends.it; hours: daily 7:30AM–2AM) they do it very well: a free buffet assures the bar is crowded and enticing.

People-watching is hardly the only attraction of **Ombre Rosse Caffè (28)** (P.za Sant'Egidio 12-13, 06-588.41.55, *www.ombrerossecaffe.it*; call for hours), known for its late-night jazz and blues sets and art exhibitions in the back room. Nurse a *birra*, Campari, or Pinot Grigio in a superb spot of the city. Located in the former parsonage of Santa Maria in Trastevere, the gastropub **Artù Caffè (29)** (Largo M.D. Fumasoni Biondi 5, 06-588.03.98; call for hours) is graced with stained glass windows, wood paneling, and great beer on tap; it also offers good pastas, sandwiches, and hamburgers.

A popular beer hall, **La Scala (30)** *(P.za della Scala 58-61, 06-580.37.63, www.ristorantelascala.it; hours: daily 12PM–12:30AM)* is always crowded, a testament to its appeal.

On the outskirts of Trastevere near **Villa Sciarra (12)**, trendy **RipArte Caffè (31) (€-€€)** *(Via degli Orti di Trastevere 1, 06-586.11, www.riparte.com; hours: daily 10:30AM–11:30PM)*, with its Italian-fusion and seafood specials, is a dinner and late-night hot spot. A bit farther south is another appealing restaurant, **Il Cortile (32) (€€)** *(Via Alberto Mario 26, 06-580.34.33, www.ristoranteilcortile.it; call for hours)*. A vegetable appetizer buffet, traditional Italian entrées, and yummy desserts are only part of the draw. Outdoor dining and the friendly owners also make the experience exceptional.

WHERE TO SHOP

Art in shoemaking characterizes the footwear at **Joseph Debach (33)** *(Vicolo dei Cinque 19, 06-556.27.56, www.josephdebach.com)*. Each pair is unusual, some with

uncommon materials worked into the design—such as newspapers, wheels, or cobblestones. High-fashion designer fabrics in silk, linen, and cotton are the raw materials of the romantic ready-to-wear and custom-made women's clothing at **Scala Quattordici (34)** *(Via della Scala 14, 06-588.35.80)*.

The **Almost Corner Bookshop (35)** *(Via del Moro 45, 06-583.69.42)* is one of Rome's best English-language bookstores; the ivy-covered exterior is nearly as appealing as the cozy inside, which has a wide variety of books. Plaster architectural embell-

ishments from **Eredi Baiocco (36)** *(Via della Luce 3A, 06-581.88.54; hours: M–F 9AM–5:30PM, Sa 9AM–1PM)* ornament some of Europe's most exclusive hotels. Bas-reliefs, statues, ceiling medallions, cornices, columns, pedestals, and many other types of decorating pieces can be shipped or wrapped up and carried home.

The famous **Porta Portese Flea Market (37)** *(Viale Trastevere, from Porta Portese to Trastevere Station, Sundays only, 7AM–2PM)*, the black market during World War II, may be the greatest flea market in Europe.

Unique objects, modern clothes, the occasional great retro frock, odd items, and all sorts of bargains—and junk!—make it a shopper's paradise. Antiques, old laces and linens, costume jewelry, and bric-a-brac are concentrated in Via Ippolito Nievo. **Pandora della Malva (38)** *(P.za San Giovanni della Malva 3, 06-581.34.06, www.pandoradellamalva.it)* is a treasure trove of Venetian glass, from exquisite vases to beautiful necklaces; it also sells ceramics and offbeat, inexpensive jewelry. **Officina della Carta (39)** *(Via Benedetta 26b, 06-589.55.57; hours: M–Sa 10AM–1PM, 3:30PM–7:30PM, closed 2 wks Aug)* is a true old-world stationery store. Handmade paper, cards, diaries, photo albums, and much more are made with a rare beauty and precision. Custom-made stationery, business cards, and invitations can be ordered.

WHERE TO STAY

A 17th-century palazzo turned into suites, **Residence in Trastevere (38) (€-€€)** *(Vicolo Moroni 35-36, 06-808.33.75, www.residencetrastevereroma.com, minimum one week)* is full of lovely details, such as open beams and a roof terrace with views of Gianicolo Hill. Once a 17th-century cloister, **Hotel Santa Maria (39) (€-€€€)** *(Vicolo del Piede 2, 06-589.46.26, www.htlsantamaria.com)* is well protected from the noise of Trastevere's partylovers. The small but warmly furnished rooms look out over the courtyard with its orange trees, and the staff is very helpful. Attractive, with comfortable rooms, **La Cisterna (40) (€)** *(Via della Cisterna 8, 06-581.72.12, www.cisternahotel.it)* is a small hotel in the heart of medieval Trastevere; the lovely courtyard has a fountain. **Hotel Trastevere (41) (€)** *(Via Luciano Manara 24A-25, 06-581.47.13 www.hoteltrastevere.net)* is a modest hotel with open-faced brick walls and small but pleasant rooms with a view of the market. **Residenza Santa Maria (42) (€-€€€)** *(Via dell'Arco di San Calisto 20, 06-58.33.51.03, www.residenzasantamaria.com)*, a charming hotel on a cobblestone street, offers a beautiful courtyard, spacious rooms, ample breakfasts, and lovely décor that includes original beams and archaeological finds.

GIANICOLO

B: Botanic Gardens—23, 125, 280, 630, 780;
Palazzo Corsini—23, 60, 65, 125, 170, 280, 630, 780;
Bramante Tempietto—44, 75;
Garibaldi Monument—870

• SNAPSHOT •

To the north of the labyrinth of winding alleys of Trastevere is the marvelously bucolic Gianicolo Hill. The breathtaking panorama of the city vies with the beauty of the hill itself, especially its lovely Botanical Gardens. The main pathways of the hill lead to a piazza where the huge equestrian statue of Giuseppe Garibaldi stands as a monument to the man who fought for the unification of Italy and liberation from papal rule. The statue is on a terrace overlooking the city. Churches, monuments, Bramante's little temple, and the colossal fountain of the Paola Aqueduct are among the highlights of the Gianicolo. But most of all, when you've seen too many ancient ruins, when you have ceased to differentiate one ornate church from another, or when narrow, crowded streets begin to make you feel claustrophobic, the Gianicolo is the perfect remedy.

PLACES TO SEE
Landmarks:
From Trastevere, the most dramatic entrance into the Gianicolo is via the Renaissance **Porta Settimiana (2)** *(between Via della Scala and Via della Lungara)*. Via della

Lungara passes beneath the gateway, a street built by Pope Sixtus V in the 16th century to connect Trastevere to the Vatican. Several notable villas were built along this road. In his sumptuous palace **Villa Farnesina (43)** *(Via della Lungara 230, 06-68.02.72.68; hours: M–Sa 9AM–2PM, open 2nd Su of month 9AM–5PM; guided tours M, F, Sa 12:30PM)*, Agostino Chigi, the Vatican banker from Siena, entertained the high and the mighty of the 16th century. When he went bankrupt, his villa at the foot of the Gianicolo was bought by Cardinal Alessandro Farnese, who gave it its present name. Chigi was one of Raphael's important patrons, and the villa is full of stupendous, vividly colored frescoes by the master as well as others spectacularly painted by Baldassare Peruzzi.

The 17th-century Swedish Queen Christina was owner of **Palazzo Corsini (44)** *(Via della Lungara 10, 06-68.80.23.23, www.galleriaborghese.it; hours: Tu–Su 8:30AM–7:30PM)*, known at the time as Palazzo Riario. Christina was famous for her grand library, her fabulous art collection of Old Masters, her commissioning music from Scarlatti and Corelli, and her many female and male lovers, the latter of whom were clergymen. The villa was later bought by the Corsini family and today houses the **Galleria Nazionale d'Arte Antica** *(Palazzo Corsini)*, part of the national art collection.

Behind Palazzo Corsini, at the foot of Gianicolo Hill, **Orto Botanico (45)** (*Largo Cristina di Svezia 24, 06-686.41.93*) originally belonged to the Palazzo Corsini but is now the property of the University of Rome. A bamboo forest, palm trees, plants both indigenous to Italy and others from abroad, glorious flower beds, medicinal plants—all thrive in the lush, secluded splendor of the garden, where waterfalls, ponds, sculptures, and fountains add another dimension to the exotic flora.

Ascending Gianicolo Hill is a bit of a trek, but the incredible views of Rome make it worthwhile. Approaching from the south, there are a few notable landmarks along the way. **Porta San Pancrazio** (*Piazzale Aurelio*) is a lovely spot. Duck into the courtyard of **San Pietro in Montorio** to see Bramante's **Tempietto (46)** (*P.za San Pietro in Montorio, in the church's courtyard, 06-581.39.40, www.sanpietroinmontorio.it; hours: M–F 8:30AM–12PM, 3PM–4PM, Sa–Su 8:30AM–12PM*). It is, as its name indicates, a little temple, round and domed, with Classical proportions and 16 Doric columns. It marks the place where some scholars believe St. Peter was crucified (the more accepted claim is that he was martyred where St. Peter's Basilica stands). Further up the hill, the monumental

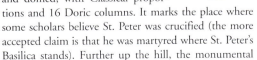

177

Fontana dell'Acqua Paola (47) *(Via Garibaldi)* is the visible manifestation of a 2nd-century aqueduct built by Emperor Trajan and restored by Pope Paul V, a Borghese—hence the change in name to Acqua Paola.

On a large, lively square, the enormous **Garibaldi Monument (48)** *(Piazzale Giuseppe Garibaldi)* commemorates Garibaldi and his Republican soldiers, who fought the French from the Gianicolo. North of the piazza is the **Anita Garibaldi Monument** *(Piazzale A. Garibaldi)*, a dramatic equestrian statue of Garibaldi's Brazilian wife, who also fought valiantly against the French. Continuing north brings you past the **Manfredi Lighthouse** *(Viale Aldo Fabrizi)*, a gift of Italian Argentinians, to **Sant'Onofrio** *(P.za Sant'Onofrio 2)*, containing the tomb of Renaissance poet Torquato Tasso.

Arts & Entertainment:

Galleria Nazionale d'Arte Antica, the notable state-owned art collection at the **Palazzo Corsini (44)** *(see page 176)* also known as **Galleria Corsini**, includes works by Rubens, Van Dyck, Caravaggio, Fra Angelico, Guercino, Guido Reni, and Murillo, among others. **Teatro Ghione (49)** *(Via delle Fornaci 37, 06-637.22.94, www.teatroghione.it; box office hours: daily 10AM–1PM, 4PM–7PM)*, beautiful and hip, is a desirable venue for well-known musicians and theater groups, both Italian and international. **Filmstudio (50)** *(Via degli Orti d'Alibert 1C, 334-178.06.32,*

www.filmstudioroma.com; call for showtimes) was a focal point in the filmmaking scene of the 1960s. Now renovated, it continues to make its mark as one of the oldest art house cinemas in Rome. It's a one-of-a-kind place for independent films, video art, and experimental pieces from the '60s.

In the converted stables next door, London art dealer and patron Lorcan O'Neill opened **Galleria Lorcan O'Neill (51)** *(Via degli Orti d'Alibert 1e, 06-68.89.29.80, www.lorcanoneill.com; hours: M–F 12PM–8PM, Sa 2PM–8PM)* in response to the burgeoning art scene in Rome. The gallery has presented exhibitions of Italian and international artistic stars, such as Luigi Ontani, Tracey Emin, Kiki Smith, and Jeff Wall.

PLACES TO EAT & DRINK
Where to Eat:

After a climb up Gianicolo Hill, have lunch (or dinner) with the locals under the pergola at **Scarpone (52)** (€€-€€€) *(Via San Pancrazio 15, 06-581.40.94, www.ristorantenteloscarpone.com; hours: Tu–Su 12:30PM–3PM, 7PM–11PM)*. Be sure to try **Antico Arco (53)** (€€-€€€) *(Piazzale Aurelio 7, 06-581.52.74, www.anticoarco.it; hours: daily 12PM–3PM, 7PM–12AM)*, a hip, minimalist eatery. The chefs do magical things with fresh seasonal produce, transforming classical Roman dishes like spaghetti *cacio e pepe* (cheese and pepper) with a surprising sauce of zucchini flowers. After a vigorous walk on the hill, **Bar Gianicolo (54) (€)** *(Piazzale Aurelio 5, 06-580.62.75; hours: Tu–Sa 6AM–1AM, Su 6AM–9PM, closed 1 wk Aug)*, by the beautiful **Porta San Pancrazio** *(Piazzale Aurelio)*, is a great pick-me-up. The *baretto* has exceptional snacks and lunch sandwiches at ridiculously low prices. Nearby, a local favorite, **Antica Pesa (55) (€€–€€€)** *(Via Garibaldi 18, 06-580.92.36, www.antica pesa.it; hours: M–Sa 7PM–12AM)*, offers traditional trattoria-style Roman food. **Terminal Gianicolo (56) (€)** *(Via Urbano VIII 16c, 06-684.0331, www.gianicolo.it; call for hours)* offers "all you can eat" pizza—but only

one type each night. The large multi-room space is family friendly, with toys for kids and two huge screens that show soccer games all night. For hungry pizza-lovers, it's perfect; for those expecting a gourmet Italian meal, steer clear.

WHERE TO STAY

Atop Gianicolo Hill in an 18th-century villa, **Grand Hotel del Gianicolo (57) (€€)** *(Viale delle Mura Gianicolensi 107, 06-58.33.55.22, www.grandhotel gianicolo.it)* offers more than rooms done in marble and appointed with Murano glass. The swimming pool,

encircled by palm trees, is spectacular, and the extraordinary view from the roof garden makes you truly feel like you're at the top of the world.

Exposed wood beams help embellish the simplicity of **Hotel la Rovere (58) (€€)** *(Vicolo di Sant'Onofrio 4-5, 06-68.80.67.39, www.hotellarovere.com)*, and some rooms have terraces. Single rooms are spare with few amenities, but doubles have A/C, heated towel racks, refrigerators, and bike rentals.

> If you're in search of more greenery, travel west to **Villa Doria Pamphilj** *(Via di San Pancrazio, B: 31, 44, 75, 710, 870)*, one of the largest parks in Rome. It's a jogger's heaven.

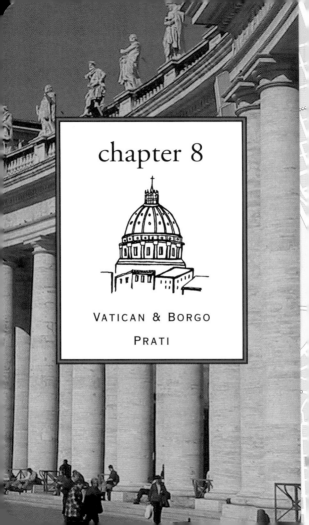

chapter 8

VATICAN & BORGO
PRATI

VATICAN & BORGO PRATI

Places to See:
1. St. Peter's Square
2. ST. PETER'S BASILICA ★
3. Vatican Gardens
4. Passetto
5. Hospital of Santo Spirito
6. Museum of Health Arts
7. Vatican Museums:
   RAPHAEL ROOMS ★
   SISTINE CHAPEL ★
20. Castel Sant'Angelo
21. Palazzo di Giustizia
22. Cinema Azzurro Scipioni

Places to Eat & Drink:
8. Caffè San Pietro
9. La Veranda
10. Velando
11. Antica Latteria Giuliani
12. Nuvolari
23. Il Matriciano
24. Ottaviani
25. Dal Toscano
26. Il Simposio
27. Cremeria Ottaviani
28. Gelateria dei Gracchi
29. Gelarmony
30. Alexanderplatz
31. The Place
32. BarBar

Where to Shop:
13. Savelli
14. Italia Garipoli
15. High-Tech d'Epoca
33. Angelo di Nepi
34. Gente
35. Vesti a stock
36. Mondadori
37. Maesano
38. Doctor Music
39. 40°
40. Costantini
41. Boccanera
42. Piazza dell'Unità Produce Market

Where to Stay:
16. Residenza Paolo VI
17. Hotel Bramante
18. Sant'Anna
19. Atlante Star
43. Hotel Colors
44. Hotel Alimandi Tunisi

★ *Top Picks*

VATICAN & BORGO

B: St. Peter's—23, 40, 62, 64;
Vatican Museums—23, 32, 34, 49, 81, 492

M: St. Peter's—A to Ottaviano-San Pietro;
Vatican Museums—A to Cipro-Musei Vaticani or
Ottaviano-San Pietro

• SNAPSHOT •

The Vatican lies on what was swampland in the 1st century BC. Emperor Caligula decided to build a circus (or stadium) there for chariot races, a project completed by his nephew Nero when he became emperor in AD 54. Ten years later, Nero began a campaign of persecution much larger than the one already being waged. Instead of chariot races, Nero's circus became the place where Christians were tarred and burned alive. It is believed that St. Peter, the apostle and first bishop of Rome (later called the pope or pontiff), was crucified in the circus and buried nearby. On his tomb in AD 326 Emperor Constantine built the first church of St. Peter, fulfilling the promise in the Gospel of St. Matthew: "You are Peter, and upon this rock I will build my church." Throughout the centuries, pilgrims continued to go to the tomb of St. Peter, the most sacred of Catholic shrines. The Borgo developed around this church, a "town" (or *burg*) to accommodate the religious tourists of the Dark Ages.

The Vatican is the smallest sovereign state in the world, with a population under 900 occupying 109 acres. Yet its political influence is felt the world over. The pope confers with world leaders and sways the political and social choices of millions of people around the globe.

The Vatican City is run as a state within a state, with its own police force (the Swiss Guard, with its plumes and exuberantly striped uniforms), a post office, Radio Vatican (which broadcasts to the world in 20 different languages), a daily newspaper *(L'Osservatore Romano)*, a publishing house, schools, an Internet domain (.va), shops, and the Vatican offices.

Pilgrims, tourists, and art lovers flock to the Vatican, irrespective of their religious leanings, to appreciate the beauty and majesty of its many masterpieces. The highlights are Piazza San Pietro, St. Peter's Basilica, the Vatican Museums, and the Vatican Gardens. The streets outside Piazza San Pietro—the Borgo—are full of restaurants, shops, and hotels.

DRESS CODE
The strictly enforced dress code in all parts of the Vatican City forbids shorts, short skirts, bare shoulders and knees, and exposed midriffs.

PLACES TO SEE
Landmarks:

Nowhere in the world is the extravagant wealth of the Catholic Church as evident as in the Vatican City. From the moment you enter **St. Peter's Square (1)**, you are overwhelmed by the grandeur and enormity of the place. An oval bound by two semicircular colonnades, the Piazza San Pietro was designed by Bernini in the mid-17th century. St. Peter's Square leads directly to ★**ST. PETER'S BASILICA (2)** *(P.za San Pietro, Vatican Switchboard 06-69.82, Vatican Tourism Office 06-69.88.23.50, www.saintpetersbasilica.org, www.vatican.va, www.vaticanstate.va; hours: Basilica Apr–Sept 7AM–7PM, Oct–Mar 7AM–6PM; Treasury Museum Apr–Sept 9AM–6:15PM, Oct–Mar 9AM–5:15PM; Grottoes Apr–Sept 7AM–6PM, Oct–Mar 7AM–5PM; Cupola Apr–Sept 8AM–6PM, Oct–Mar 8AM–4:45PM).* Of Rome's 650 or so churches, about 350 of them are in the city center; none is as opulent, magnificent, or awe-inspiring as St. Peter's. It is the heart of the Vatican State and the tomb of the founder of the Roman Catholic Church.

TOP PICK!

Construction on the present St. Peter's began in 1506 when Pope Julius II finally ordered the demolition of the original 4th-century church erected by Emperor Constantine, in a state of collapse after twelve centuries. For the next hundred years, a series of artists and architects worked on the new basilica, each master changing the plans according to his vision. The main debate was whether the church should be shaped in the form of a Greek cross (four arms of equal length) or a Latin cross (a longer vertical segment with a shorter crossbar). Bramante, the original 1506 designer, envisioned a church similar to Santa Sophia, the Greek Orthodox cathedral in Constantinople, so his plan called for a Greek cross layout. When Raphael took over the project in 1514, he changed it to a Latin cross. Michelangelo, in 1547, switched it back to a Greek cross. He also created the plans for the present **dome of St. Peter's**, completed in 1590, 26 years after his death, and still the highest point in the city. Finally, in 1607, Pope Paul V made the decision: a Latin cross it would be, and Carlo Maderno was the architect to do it. The basilica was finally opened on November 18, 1626.

Five front doors lead into St. Peter's, the central ones taken from the original 4th-century church. The last door on the right is the **Porta Santa** (Holy Door), which is opened by the Pope only in Holy Years (every 25 years) and left open throughout that year. By the Holy Door, in a chapel to the right of the nave, is Michelangelo's famous marble masterpiece, the **Pietà**, which he sculpted when he was 25. Throughout the church and its chapels are works by master artists, including Bernini, Canova, and Algardi.

You can go up into Michelangelo's **dome** by climbing hundreds of stairs or taking the small elevator to the roof of the basilica, then climbing 320 slippery marble steps.

But once you've made it up there, what a breathtaking view! The Vatican Gardens, Rome, the world beyond—the panorama is magnificent.

> **Survivor's Guide to the Vatican**
>
> Keep a few things in mind when you set out for the Vatican. Noon is the least crowded time to go; Saturdays, Mondays, and religious holidays are especially crowded. Marble stairs, particularly in the dome, can be treacherous. Most of the areas—the Sistine Chapel excluded—are not air-conditioned, so it can get terribly hot. Some interesting details (like the ceiling of the Sistine Chapel) can't be seen up close. And be forewarned: the museum pieces are not well labeled at all. Therefore, take along the following essentials:
>
> - comfortable, nonslip shoes
> - bottled water
> - binoculars
> - guidebook specific to the museums

To the west of the basilica are the **Vatican Gardens (3)** *(Viale Vaticano)*, comprising 58 of the 109 acres of the Vatican. They can be visited only by taking a two-hour guided tour *(must be booked a week in advance via fax 06-69.88.51.00, info 06-69.88.46.76; pick up tickets 2–3 days before visit at Vatican info office, P.za San Pietro,* left of basilica; tours depart from Vatican Museums, proper attire required; for more info, Vatican Tourism Office, 06-69.88.23.50). The grounds include formal Renaissance gardens with fountains and statues, tall palm trees, massive oaks, winding paths, and wildly colorful flowers.

Running along the north side of **Via della Conciliazione** is the **Passetto (4)** *(between Vatican and Castel Sant'Angelo)*, or Vatican Corridor, a covered above-ground escape route built during the Middle Ages for popes and their retinues to escape to the more fortified **Castel Sant'Angelo (20)** *(see page 195)*.

Nearby, the **Hospital of Santo Spirito (5)** *(Borgo Santo Spirito 2, 06-683.51; hours: Chapel, daily 8:30AM–2PM)* has been taking care of abandoned babies and sick indigents since the early 13th century, when Pope Innocent III had a dream in which an angel took him to the Tiber to drag up the dead bodies of unwanted babies. The hospital's **Museum of Health Arts (6)** *(Lungotevere in Sassia 3, 06-689.30.51, 06-678.78.64, www.museiscientificiroma.eu/artesanitaria/info.html; hours: M, W, F 10AM–12PM, closed Aug)* has breathtaking frescoed walls, done in the Renaissance, as well as a room full of gruesome medical instruments.

Arts & Entertainment:

The patronage of popes over the centuries has resulted in an important collection of Classical and Renaissance art in the **Vatican Museums (7)** *(entrance to the museum complex in Viale del Vaticano, 06-69.88.38.60, www.vatican.va; hours: Mar–Oct M–F 8:45AM–4:45PM/last entrance at*

3:20PM, Sa 8:45AM–1:45PM/last entrance 12:20PM, Nov–Feb M–Sa 8:45AM–1:45PM/last entrance 12:20PM, open last Su of month 9AM–2PM/last entrance at 12:30PM, free). Archaeological discoveries made in central Italy are also included in the collection, as are Egyptian, Etruscan, Greek, and Roman antiquities. The Etruscan Museum, Egyptian Museum, Pio-Christian Museum, Gregorian Profane Museum, and Vatican Library are among numerous others on the museum campus, all containing fascinating works. Several should not be missed.

TOP PICK! The frescoes in the ★**RAPHAEL ROOMS**, Renaissance masterpieces, were created by Raphael and his students when Pope Julius II commissioned the master artist to decorate the four rooms of his private apartments. This work took over 16 years to finish and gave Raphael a reputation as illustrious as that of Michelangelo (who was working at the time on the Sistine Chapel, which he completed in four years, frescoing atop a special scaffolding). Raphael died before the work was finished, but his students fulfilled the master's vision.

TOP PICK! The ★**SISTINE CHAPEL** is the main chapel of the Vatican Palace. Some of the most masterful artists of the 15th and 16th centuries created the frescoes on its walls, including Perugino, Ghirlandaio, Botticelli, and Signorelli. Michelangelo painted *The Last Judgment*, the fresco on the altar wall, as well as the chapel ceiling. The ceiling's central panels depict the Creation of the World, The Creation and Fall of Man, and The Story of Noah. The

Classical Sibyls and Old and New Testament stories appear in the surrounding panels.

PLACES TO EAT & DRINK
Where to Eat:

Caffè San Pietro (8) (€) *(Via della Conciliazione 40-42, 06-687.14.72; call for hours)*, founded in 1775, is the second oldest Roman café operating today (after Caffè Greco in Piazza di Spagna, *see page 52*). As the only bar-restaurant in **Via della Conciliazione**, it is full of customers, not a few of whom are clergy and officials from the Vatican. It's good for an Italian breakfast of cappuccino and *cornetti* (croissants) before a visit to the Vatican, or a lunch of Roman fare.

In the 15th-century Palazzo della Rovere near the Vatican, **La Veranda (9) (€€-€€€)** *(Hotel Columbus, Borgo di Santo Spirito 73, off Via della Conciliazione, 06-687.29.73, www.laveranda.net; hours: Tu–Su 12:30PM–3:15PM, 7:30PM–11:15PM)* is delicious, romantic, and, with its original Pinturicchio frescoes, eye-popping. At **Velando (10) (€€)** *(Borgo Vittorio 26, 06-68.80.99.55, www.ristorantevelando.it; call for hours, closed Su)* the owner is from Lombardy and the chef is from Apulia. In an Italian version of cultural diversity, North and South hit it off, and the food is fabulous. **Antica Latteria Giuliani (11) (€)** *(Borgo Pio 48, 06-68.80.39.55; call for hours)* is a good spot for breakfast or a quiet afternoon coffee.

Bars & Nightlife:

A typical Roman bar, **Nuvolari (12)** *(Via degli Ombrellari 10, 06-68.80.30.18; hours: M–Sa 6:30PM–2AM)* attracts locals as well as tourists for evening drinks.

WHERE TO SHOP

Via della Conciliazione, outside **St. Peter's Basilica (2)**, is full of shops selling religious articles and Vatican souvenirs. The place for religious mosaics is **Savelli (13)** *(Via Paolo VI 27–29, 06-68.30.70.17, www.savellireligious.com)*. Exquisite hand-embroidered lace and table and bed linens your grandmother would have loved are the specialty of **Italia Garipoli (14)** *(Borgo Vittorio 91, 06-68.80.21.96)*. They'll also mend lace. **High-Tech d'Epoca (15)** *(P.za Capponi 7, 06-687.21.47, www.htdepoca.it)*, run by an architect, specializes in antiques and office furniture from the early 1900s.

WHERE TO STAY

Once a monastery, **Residenza Paolo VI (16)** (€-€€) *(Via Paolo VI 29, 06-684.870, www.residenzapaolovi.com)* is a fine hotel overlooking the Vatican. The double rooms in what were monks' quarters are small but elegant, and the junior suites enjoy a beautiful view of the papal city. The former home of Renaissance architect Domenico Fontana, **Hotel Bramante (17)** (€-€€) *(Vicolo delle Palline 24, 06-68.80.64.26, www.hotelbramante.com)* has been beautifully restored, the rooms decorated with antique furnishings, and the sense of history underscored by the serene atmosphere.

The breakfast room frescoes and the courtyard fountain are some of the touches that give the small hotel **Sant'Anna (18) (€€)** *(Borgo Pio 133, 06-68.80.16.02, www.hotelsantanna.com)* its chic mark of distinction. The rooms are large, with small terraces adding allure to the top-floor spaces. The most exclusive of the hotels around the Vatican is the **Atlante Star (19) (€€-€€€)** *(Via Vitelleschi 34, 06-686.38, www.atlantestarhotel.com)*. Rooms are furnished with antiques, and the marble bathrooms have hot tubs. This sumptuous hotel has a huge roof garden with a view to die for.

PRATI

B: 23, 34, 40, 49, 70, 87, 280, 590, 926
M: A to Lepanto or Ottaviano-San Pietro

• SNAPSHOT •

Northeast of the Vatican and the Borgo lies Prati, a middle-class residential neighborhood of Rome. *Prati* means "fields." When Rome became the capital of unified Italy in 1871, the fields and meadows north of the Vatican were used to create housing for the staff of the new state. Prati became a bourgeois quarter of residences for people who worked in parliament and the ministries across the river. Elegant and peaceful, it has none of the vestiges of past eras—no ancient ruins, no narrow medieval streets, no Renaissance or Baroque garnishes. Rather, it reflects the contemporary life of middle-class Romans. It's also a shopping area, mostly along Via Cola di Rienzo and around Via Ottaviano. When the splendor of the Vatican's riches and the jostling of its crowds become unbearable, take a stroll through Prati, stop for lunch or an ice cream, and find some repose. Or go straight to Castel Sant'Angelo, Hadrian's fortress mausoleum that has been a prison as well as a papal refuge, to catch the beautiful Roman sunset.

PLACES TO SEE
Landmarks:

In the residential Prati district, the most spectacular landmark is **Castel Sant'Angelo (20)** *(Lungotevere Castello 50, entrance through gardens on right, 06-681.91.11, www.castelsantangelo.com; hours: Tu–Su 9AM–7:30PM/last entrance 6:30PM)*. Built in the 2nd century as Emperor Hadrian's mausoleum, it underwent a series of changes in function: fortress, prison, papal residence. It formed part of Emperor Aurelian's wall encircling the city, and was a place of refuge for popes who were whisked there from the Vatican through the fortified **Passetto (4)** *(see page 189)* during various sackings of Rome. Today it is a museum chronicling the history of the fortress and serving as a space for temporary exhibitions. Hadrian had a spiral ramp built that leads to the upper terraces, where you can see fabulous views of the city and its surroundings.  It is from the top of **Castel Sant'Angelo (20)** that Tosca jumps to her death in the Tiber when she discovers, in the final scene of Puccini's opera, that the villain has murdered her lover, Mario.

The **Palazzo di Giustizia (21)** *(P.za Cavour, not open to the public)*, the "Palace of Justice" law courts, built between 1889 and 1910 to right the injustices of papal rule, has not been immune to the corruption that has plagued Rome since Romulus killed Remus. Its façade is ornate and pompous, decorated with statues of Italian men of law and topped with a bronze chariot. Romans nicknamed it the *Palazzaccio*—the "big ugly palace."

Arts & Entertainment:

When you max out on antiquities, there's always the movies. **Cinema Azzurro Scipioni (22)** *(Via degli Scipioni 82, 06-39.73.71.61, www.silvanoagosti.it; call for showtimes, closed M, T, Th)* is a quirky movie theater with airplane seats. It shows films not seen elsewhere and classics, usually in the original language. All summer (June–September) in the gardens of **Castel Sant'Angelo (20)**, a literary festival offers an opportunity to see Romans relaxing. Besides bookstalls and readings, there are also movies and outdoor eateries.

PLACES TO EAT & DRINK
Where to Eat:

Il Matriciano (23) (€€-€€€) *(Via dei Gracchi 55, 06-321.30.40/06-321.23.27; hours: daily 12:30PM–3PM, 8PM–11:30PM, closed in Aug & W in winter, Sa in summer)* is a big, bright, friendly (albeit expensive) place with specialty meat dishes and a great antipasto plate with prosciutto, cheese, artichoke croquettes, and more. The pastas are delectable, and the *millefoglie*, a Napoleon layered with whipped cream, is divine. **Ottaviani (24)** (€) *(Via Paolo Emilio 9-11, 06-324.33.02, www.ottavinidal1961.com; call for hours)* offers you a wide range of choices for your pizza toppings.

For Tuscan specialties, go to **Dal Toscano (25)** (€€) *(Via Germanico 58, 06-39.72.57.17/06-39.72.33.73, www.ristorantedaltoscano.it; hours: Tu–Su 12:30PM–3PM, 8PM–11:15PM)*, a popular eatery. An offshoot of **Costantini (40)**, one of Rome's best wine shops *(see page 199)*, **Il Simposio (26)** (€€€) *(P.za Cavour 16, 06-321.15.02/06-320.35.75, www.pierocostantini.it; hours: M–Sa 12:30PM–3PM, 7:30PM–11PM; wine bar M–Sa 12:30PM–3PM, 6PM–11PM, book ahead)* serves Roman dishes as delectable as its wines. Its Art Nouveau décor, walnut tables, and small but exceptional menu make this romantic little restaurant a sure thing.

Ice cream parlors worth a visit: **Cremeria Ottaviani (27)** (€) *(Via Leone IV 83-85, 06-37.35.20.03; closed W, call for hours)*; **Gelateria dei Gracchi (28)** (€) *(Via dei Gracchi 272, 06-321.66.68, www.gelateriadeigracchi.com; hours: Su–Th 12PM–12AM, F–Sa 12PM–12:30AM)*; and **Gelarmony (29)** (€) *(Via M. Colonna 34, 06-320.23.95; call for hours)* are sure to please the *gelato* lover.

Bars & Nightlife:

Alexanderplatz (30) *(Via Ostia 9, 10AM–2PM: 06-39.72.18.67, after 6PM: 06-39.74.21.71, www.alexanderplatz.it; hours: doors open 8PM, live concerts Su–Th 9:45PM, F–Sa 10:30PM)* is one of Italy's best jazz clubs, featuring the finest Italian and international jazz musicians. Another good jazz club is **The Place (31)** *(Via Alberico II 27-29, 06-68.30.71.37, www.theplace.it; call for hours)*, which showcases top-notch musicians. Stylish and hip, **BarBar (32)** *(Via Ovidio 17, 06-68.30.84.35; hours: Tu–Sa 10PM–4AM, Su 8PM–2AM, closed Jun–Aug)* is a lounge with good cocktails, subdued music, and a low-key clientele.

WHERE TO SHOP
Via Cola di Rienzo is a major shopping street in Prati. Clothing shops include ready-to-wear designer boutiques such as Max Mara, Calvin Klein, and Carla G., as well as stores like Diesel and Benetton. **Angelo di Nepi (33)** *(Via Cola di Rienzo 267, 06-322.48.00, www.angelodinepi.it; call for hours)* wins raves for Italian styling of women's fashion and richly-hued fabrics. **Gente (34)** *(Via Cola di Rienzo 277, 06-321.15.16, www.genteroma.com)* promotes new designers and stocks well-known labels. For designer duds at discounts of 30 to 50%, check out **Vesti a stock (35)** *(Via Germanico 170a, 06-322.43.91)*. **Mondadori (36)** *(P.za Cola di Rienzo 81, 06-322.01.88, www.inmondadori.it; hours: M–F 9:30AM–8PM, Sa 9:30AM–8:30PM, Su 10AM–1:30PM, 4PM–8PM, closed in Aug)* is an Italian bookseller chain with a good stock of CDs and DVDs.

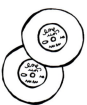

Maesano (37) *(P.za Cola di Rienzo 29, 06-321.56.74, www.maesano.it)* sells divine bed sheets and table linens. Jazz aficionados will love **Doctor Music (38)** *(Via dei Gracchi 41-43, 06-320.05.43)*; other musical genres are represented as well, in CDs and vinyl.

Vintage clothes and various *oggetti insoliti* capture the fancy at **40° (39)** *(Via Virgilio 1, at corner of Via Boezio, 06-68.13.46.12)*. **Costantini (40)** *(P.za Cavour 16, 06-320.35.75, www.pierocostantini.it; hours: M 4:30PM–8PM, Tu–Sa 9AM–1PM, 4:30PM–8PM, closed in Aug)* is one of Rome's best wine shops. The cellar master helps you choose common or rare wines from all of Italy's 20 regions. Check out the shoes (Italian, of course!) at nearby **Boccanera (41)** *(Via Vittoria Colonna 19, 06-320.44.56, www.boccanera.it)*. If you love browsing through lively farmers' markets, the **Piazza dell'Unità Produce Market (42)** *(P.za dell'Unità, 06-06.06; hours: M–Sa 7AM–2PM)* has great stuff. Its stalls sell everything from fresh mozzarella, aromatic basil leaves, and fabulous smoked cold cuts to fish, meat, and Rome's favorite—zucchini flowers.

WHERE TO STAY

Bright primary colors enliven the hostel accommodations at **Hotel Colors (43) (€)** *(Via Boezio 31, 06-687.40.30, www.colorshotel.com)*. Some rooms share baths, and the dorm room sleeps five.

With its reproductions of classical statuary and its roof garden, the family-run **Hotel Alimandi Tunisi (44) (€€)** *(Via Tunisi 8, 06-39.72.39.41, www.alimanditunisi.com, www.alimandi.it)* is pleasant and airy. It has a restaurant, gym, and plenty of spacious lounges. The rooms are large and amply furnished.

INDEX

40° 183, 199
Abbey of the Three
  Fountains 159
Agata e Romeo 75, 87
Agustarello 141, 154
Ai Tre Scalini 95, 100
Al Bric 30, 51
Al Pompiere 30, 52
Al Vino Al Vino 75, 88
Albergo Santa Chiara ... 30, 45
Albertina 56, 69
Aleph Hotel 56, 69
Alexanderplatz .. 105, 183, 197
Alexanderplatz Jazz
  Festival 105
Alibi 141, 155
Almost Corner
  Bookshop 161, 172
Alvaro al Circo
  Massimo 141, 148
Angelo di Nepi 183, 198
Anita Garibaldi
  Monument 161, 178
Antica Biblioteca 29, 36
Antica Latteria
  Giuliani 183, 191
Antica Locanda 76, 89
Antica Pesa 161, 180
Antico Arco 161, 179
Antico Tevere 161, 169
Antiquarium
  Comunale 95, 106
Antiquarium Forense 117,
  132, 134
Appian Way .. 95, 110, 113, 115
Apuleius 141, 148
Ara Pacis 55, 58
Aracoeli Stairway . 117, 121, 122
Arch of Constantine .. 117, 132
Arch of Dolabella 103
Arch of Drusus 95, 113
Arch of Septimius
  Severus 117, 129, 130
Arch of Titus ... 111, 117, 127,
  131, 132, 136
Art Cafè 55, 73
Art'è 30, 44
Arte Colosseo 96, 108
Artù Caffè 161, 170
Aspecifico Atelier
  Myriam B 75, 93
Assunta Madre 30, 51
Aston 56, 69
Atlante Star 183, 193
Aula Ottagona 75, 81
Aurelian Wall 58, 67, 110,
  111, 113, 114, 152
Aventine 114, 118, 134,
  136, 141, 143-150, 151, 156
Baptistery 98

201

Bar Canova 55, 61
Bar della Pace 29, 37
Bar Farnese 30, 51
Bar Gianicolo 161, 180
BarBar 183, 198
Basilica Julia 117, 130
Basilica of Constantine and
  Maxentius 117, 131
Baths of Caracalla 27, 95,
  110-15
Battistoni 55, 62
Bernini's elephant 41, 45
Bibli 161, 167
Big Hilda Café 161, 170
Big Mama 161, 168
Bioparco 55, 71
Bloom 29, 37
Boat Fountain 55, 60
Bocca della Verità 143, 145
Boccanera . . 141, 156, 183, 199
Bohemien 75, 88
Borgo 183, 184-193, 194
Borini 30, 52
Brioni 56, 69
Café Café 95, 107
Café de Paris 55, 68
Café Friends 161, 170
Caffè Capitolino 117, 125
Caffè Greco 55, 62
Caffè Latino 141, 155
Caffè San Pietro 183, 191
Caffè Sant'Eustachio . . . 29, 40,
  44

Campidoglio 23, 77, 117,
  119-125, 126
Campo dei Fiori 14, 29,
  46-53
Capitoline 27, 117, 118,
  119-125, 129, 131, 143, 144,
  157
Capitoline Museums 27,
  117, 123, 157
Caracalla 27, 95, 110-15
Caruso Café de Oriente . . . 141,
  155
Casa Banzo 30, 53
Casa Bleve 29, 37
Casa dei Crescenzi . . . 141, 144
Casa della Fornarina . . 161, 164
Casa-Museo Giorgio
  De Chirico 55, 60
Case Romane del Celio . 95, 103
Caserma dei Vigili della VII
  Coorte 161, 165
Castel Sant'Angelo . 22, 31, 183,
  189, 194, 195, 196
Catacombs of Domitilla . 95, 115
Catacombs of
  San Callisto 95, 115
Catacombs of
  San Sebastiano 95, 115
Celio 77, 95, 102-109,
  110, 114, 127, 134, 135, 136
Centrale Montemartini . . 141, 157
Centrum 95, 107
Checchino dal 1887 . . 141, 154
Checco er Carettiere . . 161, 169

202

Chiesa Nuova	29, 33
Chiostro dei Genovesi	161, 167
Cinema Azzurro Scipioni	183, 196
Circo Massimo	102, 110, 135, 141, 143, 146, 148
Città Universitaria	91
Clamur	141, 148
Claudio Sano	75, 93
Clivio di Scauro	95, 104
Cloaca Maxima	50
Colosseum	22, 27, 31, 41, 86, 107, 108, 109, 111, 117, 126-134, 135
Columbarium of Pomponius Hylas	95, 113
Column of Marcus Aurelius	29, 42
Coming Out	95, 107
Confetteria Moriondo e Gariglio	30, 44
Cordonata	117, 122, 123, 125
Costantini	183, 197, 199
Crab	95, 106
Cremeria Ottaviani	183, 197
Crypta Balbi	29, 48
Cryptoporticus	117, 137
Curia	117, 130
Da Baffetto	29, 36
Da Vittorio	161, 169
Dal Bolognese	55, 61
Dal Toscano	183, 197
Degli Effetti	30, 44
Dierre Bijoux	96, 101
Divinare	141, 155
Doctor Music	183, 198
Dome of St. Peter's	147, 187
Domus Augustana	117, 138, 139
Domus Aurea	75, 86, 133, 135, 137
Domus Flavia	117, 138, 139
Domus Septimius Severus	117, 138
Doney	55, 68
Doppia Coppia	161, 169
Eredi Baiocco	161, 172
Esquilino	15, 19, 21, 75, 77, 84-89
Ex-Magazzini	141, 158
F.I.S.H.	75, 87
Farnese Gardens	117, 137
Feltrinelli International	75, 82
Ferrazza	75, 92
Fiddler's Elbow	75, 88
Filmstudio	161, 178
Flowerome	76, 83
Fontana dell'Acqua Paola	161, 178
Fori Imperiali Cavalieri	117, 134
Formula 1	75, 92
Foro Italico	20, 23
Forty Seven	142, 149
Forum	27, 85, 102, 111, 117, 118, 123, 126-139, 149
Forum of Augustus	117, 129

203

Forum of Julius Caesar ... 117, 128
Forum of Nerva 117, 129
Forum of Trajan 128
Fosse Ardeatine 95, 115
Fountain of the Bees 66
Fountain of the
  Four Rivers 29, 32
Fountain of the Tortoises ... 29, 47, 48
Galleria Alberto Sordi ...29, 42
Galleria Arte e Pensieri .. 95, 105
Galleria Borghese 27, 55, 71, 73
Galleria Borghese
  Museum Shop 56, 73
Galleria Corsini 178
Galleria Lorcan O'Neill 161, 179
Galleria Nazionale d'Arte
  Antica ... 67, 161, 176, 178
Galleria Pino Casagrande ... 75, 91
Galleria SALES 95, 106
Galleria Spada 29, 48, 50
Galleria Termini/GATE ... 75, 87
Garibaldi Monument 161, 175, 178
Gelarmony 183, 197
Gelateria dei Gracchi .. 183, 197
Gente 183, 198
Gesù 29, 42
Ghetto 14, 29, 46-53, 118

Gianicolo 77, 146, 161, 174, 175-181
Gina 55, 61
Goa Club 141, 158
Grand Hotel
  de la Minerve 30, 45
Grand Hotel del Gianicolo .. 162, 180
Gregory's 55, 62
Gruppo Storico Romano ... 95, 114
Gutenberg al Colosseo .. 96, 108
Habana Café 30, 44
Harmonia Mundi 96, 108
Hasekura 75, 87
High-Tech d'Epoca ... 183, 192
Historic Museum of the
  Liberation of Rome .. 95, 100
Hospital of Santo Spirito .. 164, 183, 189
Hostaria dell'Orso 29, 36
Hotel Abitart 142, 158
Hotel Albergo del Senato . 30, 45
Hotel Alimandi Tunisi .. 183, 200
Hotel Aventino 142, 150
Hotel Bramante 183, 192
Hotel Campo de' Fiori ... 30, 53
Hotel Capo d'Africa 96, 108
Hotel Colors 183, 200
Hotel de Russie 56, 63
Hotel Domus Aventina . 142, 150
Hotel Due Torri 30, 39
Hotel Exedra 76, 83

Hotel Forum 117, 134	Il Simposio 183, 197
Hotel Hassler 56, 64	Il Vittoriano 117, 121, 146
Hotel la Rovere 162, 181	Ilaria Miani 30, 53
Hotel Lancelot 96, 108	Imperial Fora 127, 128, 134
Hotel Marcus 939 Rome . 56, 64	Isidoro 95, 100-101
Hotel Navona 30, 39	Isola Tiberina 24, 29, 49
Hotel Portoghesi 30, 39	Italia Garipoli 183, 192
Hotel Rinascimento 30, 53	Jasmine 55, 68
Hotel San Anselmo . . . 142, 150	Joia 141, 155
Hotel Santa Maria 162, 174	Joseph Debach 161, 172
Hotel Scalinata	Josephine de Huertas
di Spagna 56, 64	& Co. 30, 38
Hotel Teatro di Pompeo . 30, 53	Keats-Shelley
Hotel Trastevere 162, 174	Memorial House 55, 60
Hotel Villa San Pio . . . 142, 150	Kolbe Hotel Rome 142, 149
House of Livia 117, 137	L'Antica Birreria Peroni . . 75, 82
House of the Vestal	L'Artigianaio Orologi 75, 89
Virgins 117, 132	La Bottega del
Huts of Romulus 117, 138	Cioccolato 75, 88
Il Boom 161, 169	La Cisterna 162, 174
Il Cortile 161, 171	La Maison 29, 37
Il Discount dell'Alta Moda . . 55, 63	La Sapienza 90, 91
Il Gelato di San Crispino . . 75, 82	La Scala 161, 171
Il Giardino degli Aranci 146	La Terrazza dell'Eden . 55, 67-68
Il Giardino di Domenico	La Rosetta 29, 43
Persiani 75, 83	La Veranda 183, 191
Il Matriciano 183, 196	La Vineria 30, 52
Il museo del Louvre 30, 52	Largo Argentina Sacred
Il Negozio Benedettino della	Precincts 29, 48
Badia Primaziale di	Lateran . . . 38, 95, 97-101, 114
Sant'Anselmo 141, 149	Le Bambole 141, 156
Il Palazzetto 56, 63	Le Gallinelle 75, 88
	Lettere Caffè 161, 168

205

Li Rioni	107
Longobardi	141, 149
Luna & L'Altra	30, 38
Maccheroni	29, 43
MACRO	20, 153
MACRO Testaccio	141, 153
Maesano	183, 198
Magazzino d'Arte Moderna	30, 44
Mamertine Prison	85, 117, 129
Manfredi Lighthouse	178
Mausoleum of Augustus	55, 59
MAXXI	20
Michel Harem	56, 69
Michelangelo's Moses	84, 86
Moma	55, 68
Mondadori	183, 198
Mondello Ottica	30, 52
Monte Testaccio	141, 152
Monti	74, 75, 84–89, 118, 127, 134, 136, 148
Mr. Brown	161, 170
Museo di Roma in Trastevere	161, 165, 167
Museo Nazionale di Roma: Terme di Diocleziano	75, 81
Museum for Contemporary Art of Rome	20, 153
Museum of Health Arts	183, 189
Museum of Jewish Culture	29, 49, 50
Museum of Musical Instruments	95, 100
Museum of Palazzo Venezia	117, 125
National Gallery of Modern Art	55, 72
National Museum of Rome—Palazzo Altemps	27, 29, 34, 48
Naumachia	95, 106
Nazca	141, 158
Né Arte Né Parte	141, 154
Nuovo Sacher	161, 168
Nuvolari	183, 192
Officina della Carta	162, 173
Oliver Glowig	55, 73
Ombre Rosse Caffè	161, 170
Orto Botanico	161, 177
Osteria del Campidoglio	141, 148
Osteria dell'Ingegno	29, 43
Ostiense	12, 140, 141, 148, 152, 157–159
Ottaviani	183, 196
Palatine	111, 116, 117, 118, 135–139, 144, 146
Palatine Museum	117, 139
Palazzo Barberini	55, 67
Palazzo Colonna	75, 80
Palazzo Corsini	161, 176, 177, 178
Palazzo dei Conservatori	123, 124
Palazzo del Quirinale	75, 79

Palazzo delle Esposizioni . . . 22, 75, 81
Palazzo di Giustizia . . . 183, 195
Palazzo Doria Pamphilj . . 29, 42
Palazzo Farnese 29, 46, 47, 51
Palazzo Madama 29, 33
Palazzo Manfredi 96, 109
Palazzo Margherita 67
Palazzo Mattei 48
Palazzo Nuovo . . 122, 123, 124
Palazzo Senatore . . . 117, 119, 122, 123
Palazzo Spada 29, 47
Palazzo Venezia 117, 120, 125, 128
Pandora della Malva . . 162, 173
Panella 75, 88
Pantheon 27, 29, 40-45, 59, 118, 123
Papà Baccus 55, 68
Parco del Colle Oppio . . . 75, 86
Parco Della Musica 20
Parco Savello . . . 141, 144, 146
Pasquino (cinema) . . . 161, 168
Pasquino (statue) 29, 33
Passetto 183, 189, 195
Pasta Museum 75, 80
Pecorino 141, 154
Piazza Barberini 55, 66, 67
Piazza dei Cavalieri di Malta 141, 147
Piazza del Campidoglio 23, 117, 119, 122, 123, 124

Piazza del Popolo 26, 55, 57, 58, 61
Piazza dell'Unità Produce Market . . . 183, 199
Piazza della Repubblica 75, 79, 81, 83
Piazza di Pietra 42
Piazza di San Giovanni in Laterano . . 23, 95, 97, 98
Piazza di San Lorenzo in Lucina 56, 63
Piazza di Spagna 11, 55, 57-64, 191
Piazza in Piscinula . . . 161, 166
Piazza Navona 22, 27, 29, 31-39
Piazza Trilussa 164
Piazza Venezia . . . 120, 121, 146
Piccola Farnesina 29, 50
Pietà 187
Pincio Gardens 55, 60, 63
Piperno 30, 52
Pizzeria Luzzi 95, 106-107
Planet Roma 141, 158
Pommidoro 75, 92
Ponte Fabricio 49
Ponte Rotto 29, 50, 145
Ponte Sisto 161, 164
Porta del Popolo 55, 58
Porta Maggiore 95, 99
Porta Pinciana 66, 71
Porta Portese Flea Market . . 101, 162, 172
Porta San Pancrazio . . 177, 180

207

Porta San Sebastiano 95, 113
Porta Santa 187
Porta Settimiana . 161, 164, 175
Portico d'Ottavia 47, 49
Prati 182, 183, 194-199
Priory of the Knights
  of Malta 147
Protestant Cemetery 60, 141, 152
Pyramid of Caius Cestius .. 141, 152
Quirinale 74, 75, 77-83, 84, 118
Radisson Blu es 76, 89
Raphaël (bar) 29, 36
Raphaël (hotel) 30, 39
Raphael Rooms ... 27, 183, 190
Relais al Senato 30, 45
Residence in Trastevere ... 162, 174
Residence Palazzo al
  Velabro 142, 149
Residenza Cellini 76, 83
Residenza in Farnese ... 30, 53
Residenza Monti 76, 89
Residenza Paolo VI ... 183, 192
Residenza Santa Maria 162, 174
Residenza Zanardelli ... 30, 39
Rhome 55, 61
RipArte Caffé 161, 171
Ristorante Césarina 55, 68
Ristorante Consolini .. 141, 148
Ristorante Mario's ... 117, 134

Roman *Insula* 122
Roseto di Roma 141, 146
Rostra 117, 130
San Benedetto in
  Piscinula 161, 167
San Cesareo 95, 111
San Clemente 95, 103
San Crisogono 161, 165
San Francesco a Ripa 161, 166
San Giovanni a Porta
  Latina 95, 111
San Giovanni in Laterano ... 22, 85, 95, 97, 98, 159
San Giovanni in Oleo ... 95, 111
San Gregorio Magno ... 95, 104
San Lorenzo 75, 90-93, 131
San Lorenzo fuori le Mura .. 75, 91
San Luca National Academy
  of Art 75, 80
San Luigi dei Francesi ... 29, 34
San Marco (church) .. 117, 120
San Marco (restaurant) .. 55, 69
San Paolo Fuori Le Mura ... 85, 98, 141, 159
San Pietro in Montorio 177
San Pietro in Vincoli 27, 75, 84, 85
San Sisto Vecchio 95, 111
San Teodoro 141, 144
Sant'Agnese in Agone ... 29, 32
Sant'Andrea della Valle .. 29, 48

Sant'Anna 183, 193
Sant'Anselmo . . . 141, 147, 149
Sant'Onofrio 178
Santa Balbina 95, 111
Santa Cecilia in
    Trastevere 161, 166
Santa Croce in
    Gerusalemme 95, 99
Santa Francesca
    Romana 117, 132, 134
Santa Lucia 29, 36
Santa Maria degli
    Angeli 75, 80, 81
Santa Maria del Popolo . . 55, 58
Santa Maria della
    Concezione 55, 67
Santa Maria della
    Consolazione . 141, 144, 148
Santa Maria della Pace . . 29, 33
Santa Maria della Vittoria . . . 55, 66
Santa Maria in
    Aracoeli 117, 121, 122
Santa Maria in
    Cosmedin 141, 145
Santa Maria in Domnica 95, 105
Santa Maria in
    Trastevere 161, 165
Santa Maria in Trivio 75, 78
Santa Maria Maggiore . . 27, 75, 84, 85, 98, 159
Santa Maria sopra
    Minerva 29, 41

Santa Prisca 142, 156
Santa Sabina 141, 146
Santi Giovanni e Paolo 103
Santi Nereo e Achilleo . . 95, 111
Santi Quattro Coronati . . 95, 99
Santo Stefano Rotondo 95, 105
Savelli 183, 192
Scala Quattordici 161, 172
Scala Santa 95, 99
Scarpone 161, 179
Scipio Tomb 95, 113
Scuderie del Quirinale . . . 75, 81
Sermoneta 55, 63
Sette 89
Shangò 141, 148
Sistine Chapel 27, 86, 164, 183, 188, 190
Sole al Pantheon 30, 45
Soul Food 96, 101
Spanish Steps 16, 27, 55, 57, 59, 60
St. Peter's Basilica . 25, 27, 146, 147, 177, 183, 185, 186-188
St. Peter's Square 22, 25, 183, 186
St. Regis Grand 76, 83
Stadium (in Palatine) 117, 138
Suggestum 55, 68
Synagogue (in Ghetto) . . 29, 49
Tabularium 123
Tarpeian Rock 117, 123, 144

Taverna Giulia 30, 51
Tazza d'Oro 29, 40, 44
Teatro Argentina 29, 51
Teatro dell'Opera 75, 81
Teatro di Documenti . . 141, 153
Teatro Ghione 161, 178
Teatro Valle 29, 35
Teatro Vascello 161, 168
Tempietto 161, 177
Temple of Aesculapius 50, 55, 71
Temple of Antonius and Faustina 117, 131
Temple of Castor and Pollux 117, 131
Temple of Claudius . . . 102, 103
Temple of Cybele 117, 137
Temple of Diana 55, 71
Temple of Hadrian 29, 42
Temple of Hercules Victor 141, 145, 149
Temple of Jupiter 117, 119, 123
Temple of Portunus . . 141, 145
Temple of Romulus . . . 117, 131
Temple of Saturn 117, 130
Temple of Vespasian 130
Temple of Vesta . . 117, 132, 145
Terme di Diocleziano . 75, 79, 81
Terminal Gianicolo . . . 161, 180
Termini Train Station . . . 12, 14, 21, 75, 87, 89
Testaccio 141, 148, 151-156, 158

Testaccio Market 141, 156
The Place 183, 197
Theatre of Marcellus 29, 49
Tomb of Cecilia Metella 95, 115
Trajan's Column 117, 128
Trajan's Markets 117, 128
Tram Tram 75, 92
Trastevere 12, 22, 25, 161, 163-174, 176
Trattoria San Teodoro 141, 147
Trattoria Tritone 75, 82
Trevi 75, 77-83
Trevi Fountain 27, 75, 78
Tridente 55, 57-64
Trimani 75, 82, 83
Trinità dei Monti 16, 59, 60, 64
Triton Fountain 66
Vatican . . 22, 25, 26, 38, 59, 85, 98, 113, 147, 176, 183-193
Vatican Gardens . 183, 185, 188
Vatican Museums . . . 113, 183, 184, 185, 189
Velando 183, 191
Vesti a stock 183, 198
Vestiti Usati Cinzia 30, 38
Via Appia Antica 114, 115
Via Bocca di Leone 55, 63
Via Borgognona 55, 59, 62
Via Cola di Rienzo 194, 198
Via dei Cappellari . . . 30, 46, 52

210

Via dei Condotti 55, 59, 62
Via dei Coronari 30, 38
Via del Babuino 57, 59, 63
Via del Corso .. 8, 19, 57, 59, 77
Via del Governo
  Vecchio 30, 36, 38
Via del Pellegrino 30, 52
Via della Conciliazione 189, 191, 192
Via della Pace 29, 37
Via della Pilotta 75, 79, 80
Via di Porta San
  Sebastiano ... 111, 113, 114
Via Frattina 55, 59
Via Giulia 20, 29, 46, 48
Via Sacra 111, 127, 131, 132, 136

Via Sannio 96, 101
Via Veneto 14, 57, 65-69
Villa Borghese 27, 55, 61, 67, 70-73
Villa Celimontana .. 95, 104, 105
Villa Doria Pamphilj ... 70, 181
Villa Farnesina 161, 176
Villa Giulia 55, 72
Villa Sciarra 161, 167, 171
Villaggio Globale 141, 153
Vinosteria 75, 92
Volpetti 141, 156
Volpetti Più 141, 154
Wall Museum 95, 113, 114
Zest 89

NOTES

NOTES

NOTES

NOTES

NOTES

PHOTO CREDITS

Cover & Chapters 2, 3, 5: © Royalty-Free/Corbis

Chapter 1: © John A. Rizzo/Photodisc Green/Getty Images

Chapter 4: © Asta Plechaviciute/Shutterstock

Chapter 6: © John A. Rizzo/Photodisc Blue/Getty Images

Chapter 7: © Karl Weatherly/Photodisc Green/Getty Images

Chapter 8: © lullabi/Shutterstock

PETER PAUPER PRESS
Fine Books and Gifts Since 1928

Our Company

In 1928, at the age of twenty-two, Peter Beilenson began printing books on a small press in the basement of his parents' home in Larchmont, New York. Peter—and later his wife, Edna—sought to create fine books that sold at "prices even a pauper could afford."

Today, still family owned and operated, Peter Pauper Press continues to honor our founders' legacy—and our customers' expectations—of beauty, quality, and value.

Barbara Taylor

big ideas for little people

About this book

Children love learning about the amazing animals that populate our world. My Big Animal World takes them on a unique journey, introducing them to hundreds of animals while exploring the diverse range of environments in which they live. Looking at how they adapt to their habitats, and discovering their surprising, often amusing habits brings these intriguing creatures to life. With its easy-to-turn spiral binding, this book is a great reference tool for school projects or homework. Adults, too, will gain a fascinating insight into the lives of the many animals with whom we share our amazing world.

Written by: Barbara Taylor
Editorial by: Simon Mugford and Hermione Edwards
Design by: Emma Surry

Copyright © 2007 St. Martin's Press
Published by
priddy books

4 Crinan Street, London, N1 9XW
A division of Macmillan Publishers Ltd.

All rights reserved, including the right of reproduction in whole or in part in any form.

Manufactured in Malaysia

Contents

Animal habitats
Pages 8-9

Mountains
Pages 10-11

Wetlands
Pages 12-15

Forests
Pages 16-19
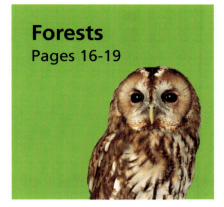

Rainforests
Pages 20-25

Grasslands
Pages 26-29
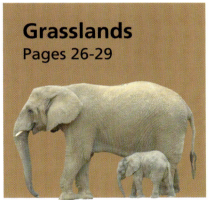

Deserts
Pages 30-33
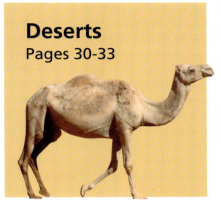

Islands
Pages 34-35
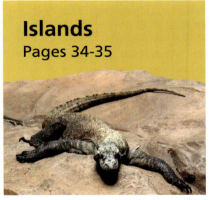

Coral reefs
Pages 36-37
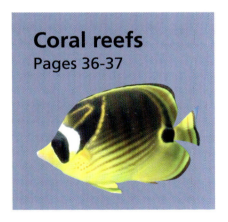

Oceans
Pages 38-41
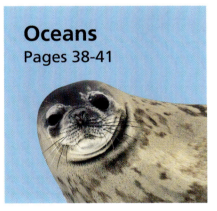

Polar areas
Pages 42-45
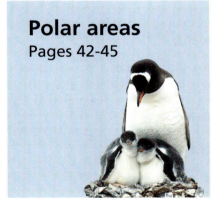

Our habitat
Pages 46-49

Animals in danger
Pages 50-53
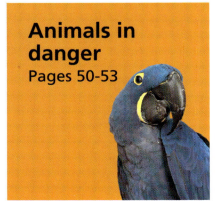

Amazing animals
Pages 54-57

Glossary
Pages 58-59

Index
Pages 60-61

Animal habitats

Animals live all over the world, in icy polar areas and cold forests as well as in baking hot deserts and steamy rainforests. The place where an animal lives is called its habitat, and each habitat has its own typical mixture of animals. The greatest variety of animals live in forest habitats, particularly in the rainforests. Only a few animals can survive in extreme habitats, such as deserts and mountains.

Mountains
Mountain tops are cold, windy places, similar to polar areas. Large birds of prey, such as eagles, are common in mountain habitats. Birds of prey can fly well in the strong mountain winds.

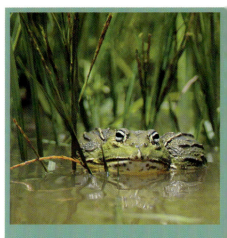

Wetlands
Wetland habitats, such as rivers, lakes and swamps, give food and shelter to animals in many different parts of the world. Wetland animals, such as otters, are good swimmers.

Islands
Cut off from the main land areas of the world, islands are often home to some very strange animals, from giant tortoises to the fearsome Komodo dragon.

In the large, open spaces of grasslands, lions usually live together in groups called prides

Forests
Forest habitats are found in the areas between the cold polar regions at either end of the globe, and the hot desert and rainforest areas around the middle. Owls are common forest animals.

Rainforests
Growing around the middle of the world, rainforests are warm all year round because they receive plenty of heat from the Sun. It is easy for animals to survive in the rainforests.

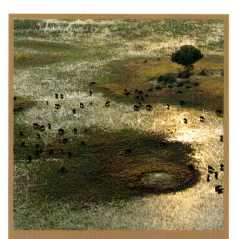
Grasslands
Grasslands grow mainly around the edges of rainforests and deserts. They are warm or hot habitats, and usually have both wet and dry seasons. Many grazing animals live here.

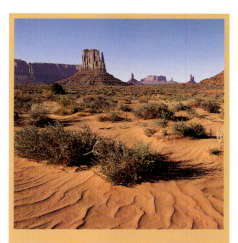
Deserts
Hardly any rain falls in deserts, and animals have to cope with dry conditions and extreme temperatures. Camels are desert animals, but many small animals live in underground burrows.

Coral reefs
Coral reefs can only form in warm oceans, because this is where the tiny coral animals that make up the reef grow. Many different animals feed among the corals, including colourful fish.

Oceans
The ocean is the biggest habitat in the world. It covers about 70 per cent of the globe. Shoreline animals, such as crabs, have to be tough as they are exposed to both air and pounding waves.

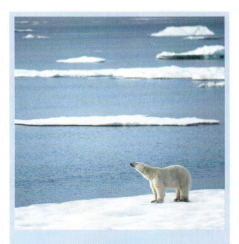
Polar areas
The polar areas at the top and bottom of the world receive less heat and light from the Sun than other parts of the world. Only very hardy animals survive the cold temperatures and winds.

Our habitat
Though we may not always be aware of them, animals surround us wherever we live – in cities as well as in the countryside. People keep animals as pets, as well as for food and wool.

Mountains

High up on mountain tops, the weather is very cold and windy, as it is in polar areas. Thick fur or feathers keep animals warm. Some animals sleep through the cold winter months, while others move down the mountain to warmer places.

Hot baths

Japanese macaques are clever monkeys. They have learnt to keep warm in winter by sitting in the hot water gushing out of volcanic springs in the mountains.

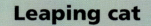

Leaping cat

The powerful snow leopard uses its long back legs to make huge leaps from rock to rock. Its big paws and strong claws help it grip slippery rocks, and its long tail helps with balance on steep mountain slopes. The snow leopard's feet have furry soles, so it can walk on snow without sinking in.

LOCATION

Climate
Temperature drops by half a degree for every 150 metres you climb, so mountain tops are often covered in snow

Habitat
Many mountain plants have hairy leaves to trap warmth and moisture, and brightly coloured flowers that attract insects

Earthwatch
Cutting down mountain forests allows soil and water to wash down the mountains, causing more floods and mudslides

10

Cows with skirts

A long hairy 'skirt' of fur keeps a yak's legs warm. Despite their large size, yaks are nimble, and are good at climbing the steep mountain slopes. In Nepal and Tibet, people keep yaks as farm animals. They use them for carrying heavy loads up and down the mountains, and also drink their milk.

Playful panda

Giant pandas live in the mountain forests of China, where there is lots of snow in winter. They love to play in the snow! Luckily, giant pandas have thick, waterproof fur, which keeps them warm and dry. Pandas are good at climbing trees. Their strong, curved claws help them grip tree trunks and branches.

Rock climber

The agile Rocky Mountain goat has hollows under its hooves that work like suction cups to grip rocks firmly. It is sure-footed, able to climb up steep rock faces and run along slippery slopes. This allows the goat to find food and avoid predators.

Sky hunter

Eagles, such as bald eagles, glide over mountain slopes, using their sharp eyes to look for prey, such as rabbits and birds. They have wide, powerful wings, and can fly well even in strong winds. They can also float on the air that rises up the mountains, which saves flapping their wings and wasting energy.

Fur coat

Wild chinchillas live high up in the Andes Mountains of South America, but they are also kept as pets. Chinchillas have very thick, soft fur to keep out the cold. Many of them have been killed for their fur, which is used to make coats and jackets.

The chamois of Europe can leap more than 6 metres forward and around 1.8 metres into the air

At 8,848 metres, Mount Everest in the Himalayas is the highest mountain on Earth

Snow leopards can bring down prey more than three times their own size

The huge condor of the Andes mountains of South America can soar through the sky for hours without flapping its wings

11

Wetlands

Wetlands provide plenty of food and shelter for a huge range of animals, especially the young of animals such as insects, frogs and fish. Enormous numbers of birds, such as flamingos and herons, nest in wetlands. Many water animals are good swimmers and have webbed feet to push them through the water easily.

White horses

These beautiful white horses live on marshlands in southern France. They are very hardy, and are able to survive hot summers and cold winters with little food to eat. Their wide hooves stop them sinking into the soft mud. The survival of these horses is threatened by the drainage and pollution of their marshland home.

LOCATION

Climate
Different types of wetlands exist in areas with varying climates, and they are sensitive to changes in local conditions

Habitat
Wetlands cover about 6 per cent of the world. They include rivers, lakes and ponds, as well as marshes, swamps and bogs

Earthwatch
Wetlands help control flooding and pollution, and protect coasts from storms. Many have already been destroyed

12

Underwater hunter

Otters swim underwater in rivers, hunting for fish and crayfish. To swim slowly, the otter moves its webbed feet up and down in a doggy-paddle movement. To move faster, the otter holds its legs close to its sides, and bends its whole body up and down. The powerful tail acts as a rudder to help the otter steer and change direction.

Paddling along

The rare manatee has a large, rounded tail, which pushes it through the water at speeds of 24 km/h. It can stay underwater for up to 15 minutes, but has to come to the surface to breathe air. Its nostrils are on the tip of its snout so it can breathe easily from the surface. Manatees munch through 75 kg of water plants in a day.

Open wide

A hippopotamus often threatens a rival by opening its mouth very wide to show off its big teeth. Hippos are very good swimmers, and can stay underwater for up to five minutes. They spend most of the day resting in lakes or rivers, and come out at night to munch the grass on lake shores or river banks.

Castle home

Beavers build a home of sticks in the middle of a pond, which they create by building a dam across a river. This home is like a castle surrounded by a moat, and is called a lodge. It helps keep predators away. Baby beavers, called kits, are born in the safety of the lodge, which has underwater entrances.

Eggs or babies?

The platypus of Australia is an extremely unusual mammal, because it lays eggs, rather than giving birth to babies like most other mammals. It has a sensitive bill, which it uses to feel for prey at the bottom of lakes and rivers. Platypuses have no teeth, so they have to crush their food between hard, ridged plates inside their bill.

Lake Baikal in Siberia is the deepest lake in the world. It contains more freshwater than North America's five Great Lakes combined

Some beaver dams are over 100 metres long and are as tall as a person. A beaver only takes ten minutes to chew down a small tree

The Amazon river is the second longest river in the world, and holds more than one-fifth of the Earth's freshwater

American alligators were once rare, but numbers are increasing. Alligators bred in captivity have been released into the wild

Snap happy

Crocodiles lurk under the water of rivers, lakes and swamps, waiting to snap up fish and other prey in their huge jaws and sharp teeth. Crocodiles have two or three times as many teeth as an adult human. These teeth keep growing, so if a tooth falls out, a new one grows through to replace it. A crocodile's teeth are not good for chewing food, so they have to swallow food whole, or tear it into chunks.

Diving jewels

To catch fish, a kingfisher dives straight down into the water, with its shiny feathers sparkling in the light. It uses its dagger-like bill to spear a fish, then carries it back to a perch above the water. After beating the fish against a hard surface, the kingfisher swallows it down whole. Kingfishers lay their eggs in tunnels that they dig in riverbanks.

Stilt legs

Herons wade through deep water on their long legs, looking for fish and frogs to catch in their sharp, pointed bill. They also have long toes, which allow them to spread out their weight. This means they can walk over mud or floating plants without sinking in.

A double life

An adult dragonfly lives in the air, but young dragonflies, called nymphs, live underwater for several years while they grow and develop. The nymphs are fierce hunters, feeding on water insects and young fish. The adults catch flying insects with their hairy legs.

Bottoms up

Mallards have skin stretched between their toes, making their feet webbed. These webbed feet work like the flippers that people wear for snorkelling, and they push the ducks quickly through the water. Mallards feed on the surface, or with their bills pointing down, under the water. Their bills are wide and flat, which allows them to strain food.

Skipping fish

The mudskipper fish can 'skip' over the mud of swamps by suddenly bending the back part of its body to push itself into the air. It also uses its fleshy fins like arms to pull itself over the surface of the mud.

Filter feeder

Flamingos use their strange bill to filter tiny plants and animals from the water. First, they dip their bill upside down into shallow water. Then they move the bottom bill and the tongue up and down. This pumps water through comb-like fringes on the sides of the top bill.

Forests

Forests and woods provide food and nesting places for a variety of animals. Their lives are closely linked to the seasons. Spring is a time for babies to be born, summer and autumn are feeding and growing seasons. Winter is for resting or moving away to warmer places.

Spiny climber

Porcupines have thousands of long, very sharp spines called quills, which give them protection from predators. One porcupine may have as many as 30,000 quills! These spiny animals use their strong claws to grip tree trunks as they search for bark to eat.

Giant deer

Moose and elk are the biggest deer in the world. They are taller than a person and weigh about as much as six people! A moose uses its overhanging top lip to tear off leaves and branches. Its long legs and wide hooves allow it to wade through snow, bogs and lakes.

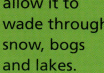

LOCATION

Climate

Winters in coniferous forests can last as long as eight months, with temperatures often below zero

Habitat

In coniferous forests, evergreen trees have leaves all year round. Deciduous trees drop their leaves in autumn

Earthwatch

Pine trees can be badly damaged by acid rain, which is caused by polluting gases mixing with water in the air

16

Furry explorer

American black bears are intelligent and curious animals that like to explore their surroundings. They are good at climbing trees. Black bears usually live alone, except for mothers with cubs. When the cubs are born, they are so tiny that their mother is over 500 times heavier than they are!

Spotted deer

Fallow deer are easy to identify because they have white spots on their coats and the males have wide, flat antlers. The males fight with their antlers in the autumn, and the strongest males win a group of females.

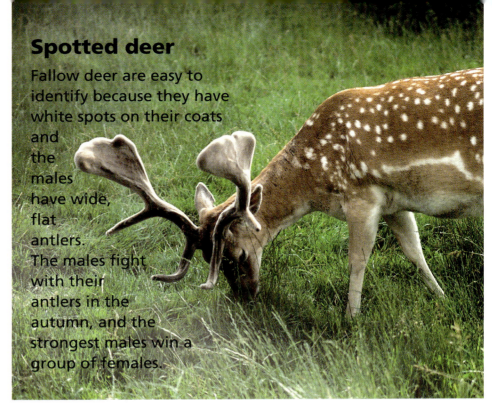

Tightrope walker

Red and grey squirrels move like tightrope walkers on the tree branches. They can climb and leap along the thinnest twigs, using their bushy tail to help them balance. Squirrels also flick their tail to signal to other squirrels.

Winter sleep

The dormouse survives the cold winter months by going into a deep sleep called hibernation. All its body processes slow down, and it lives off fat stored in its body during autumn.

Big ears

Long-eared bats make high-pitched squeaks and use their large ears to pick up the echoes as they bounce back from nearby objects. The echoes help the bats work out where things are so they can fly easily through the trees at night and find insects to eat.

Pack hunter

By hunting together in a group called a pack, wolves can kill large animals, such as deer and moose. Wolves have keen senses of smell and hearing to track their prey, and long legs to chase after their victims. They are the wild ancestors of the dogs people keep as pets.

The biggest area of forest in the world is the 'taiga' that stretches across the top of North America, Europe and Asia

Nutcrackers bury up to 4,000 seeds each autumn to feed to their young the following spring

A large oak tree is home to as many as 300 different kinds of insects

Cork is made from the bark of cork oak trees. The bark is stripped about every ten years without damaging the tree

17

Twisted bill

Crossbills are named after the way the two parts of their bill cross over at the tips. This is a good shape to lift up the scales of pine cones and reach the seeds inside. The seeds are full of goodness, and adult crossbills feed the seeds to their young.

Silent swooper

Woodland owls, such as the tawny owl (left) have short, wide, rounded wings, which allow them to fly in the small spaces between the trees. Owls can fly silently because they have fluffy fringes on their soft feathers, which muffle the sound of their wingbeats. They swoop down to catch their prey in their sharp, curved claws, called talons.

Chisel bird

Woodpeckers have a pointed, sharp bill, which they use to chisel into tree trunks to find insects to eat. They lick up the insects with a very long, sticky tongue, which can be as long as their own body.

Hide-and-seek

During the day, the whip-poor-will rests among the fallen leaves on the woodland floor. Its brown mottled feathers provide good camouflage so the bird is very hard for predators to spot. At night, the whip-poor-will flies near the ground with its mouth open to scoop up insects.

Insects such as beetles are the whip-poor-will's favourite food

Fighting beetles

Stag beetles are named after the huge jaws of the males, which look like a male deer's antlers. Males use their jaws to fight rivals, rather like human wrestlers. The beetles lock their jaws together in tests of strength. They try to lift each other into the air and throw their opponent to the ground.

Tree planter

Blue jays often bury tree seeds, such as acorns, in the autumn, and then dig them up to eat during the winter months. Many of the seeds are never eaten and grow into new trees, helping woodlands to spread.

Nest thief

The female cuckoo does not make a nest of her own. Instead, she lays her eggs in other birds' nests. When the cuckoo chick hatches out of its egg, it tips the other eggs out of the nest so it has all the food and space for itself!

Monarch marathon

Monarch butterflies fly thousands of kilometres to escape the cold winters in Canada. They fly south to forests in Mexico, where it is warmer. As they fly, the monarch butterflies glide on the wind, without flapping their wings, to save energy on their long journey.

Rainforests

Growing like a green belt around the middle of the world are wild, warm, wet forests called rainforests. Millions of different kinds of animals live in rainforests, because there is plenty of food and shelter. Most animals live near the roof of the forest where bright sunlight shines on the treetops all year round.

Night senses

The huge eyes and ears of bushbabies help them catch insects in the dark. Bushbabies are named after their strange call, which sounds like the cry of a child.

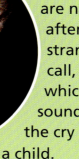

Spotted hunter

The jaguar's spotted coat allows it to hide among the leafy branches and make surprise attacks on its prey, such as wild pigs or deer. Sometimes jaguars even catch and eat crocodiles. They have very strong jaws and teeth, which can bite through bones.

LOCATION

Climate
Most rainforests can get as much as 250 cm of rainfall a year – the same height as a two-storey building

Habitat
A 6-km square area of rainforest contains as many as 1,500 flowering plants and 750 species of trees

Earthwatch
About half the world's rainforests have been cut down, and an area the size of a football pitch is destroyed every second

Clever chimps

Chimpanzees are very clever animals. They chew sticks or grass stems to make a tool for catching termites. They push the tool into a termite mound and when they pull it out, the termites are clinging to the end. Few other animals make and use tools in this way.

Super swinger

Gibbons use their very long arms to swing underneath the branches of rainforest trees. They can move at great speed, with hardly a sound. Sometimes they leap up to 15 metres.

Sluggish sloth

With claws and legs like coat hangers, sloths hang upside down from branches. They also use their long, curved claws to gather leaves and fruits or defend themselves from enemies. Sloths move incredibly slowly, and sleep for up to 18 hours a day.

Extra hand

Many rainforest animals, such as this spider monkey, have a special tail, which curls around branches like a hook. The strong tail grips so well that it works like an extra hand. Spider monkeys can even use their tails to pick leaves and fruits from the trees.

Rainforest plants and trees are a source of many of the world's most important medicines

Army ants march in huge armies of over 500,000 ants. They can overpower animals many times larger than themselves

The goliath tarantula is the biggest spider in the world. It would only just fit on a large dinner plate

The tarsier monkey has such huge eyes that one eye can weigh as much as its entire brain

Spiky lizard

The green iguana is a large lizard that lives in the jungles of Central and South America. These lizards spend most of their time high up in the trees, and their colour keeps them hidden among the leaves. They have a row of sharp, spiky scales along their back.

Magical morphos

The shiny blue wings of male morpho butterflies sparkle in the sunlight as they soar over the rainforest. The colours are produced by the way the butterflies' wings reflect the light. These wings attract females and may also dazzle enemies, giving the butterfly time to escape.

Big bill

Toucans use their long bills to reach fruits and seeds at the end of thin twigs. The brightly coloured bill is hollow inside so it is not as heavy as it looks. Toucans also use their bills to signal to other toucans.

Toucans eat fruit such as papayas

Nutcracker parrot

The strong, hooked bill of the scarlet macaw works like a nutcracker to split open tough forest nuts. Like all parrots, macaws sometimes use one of their feet to hold food up to their mouth.

Ant farmers

Leafcutter ants grow their own food in an underground nest. The ants bite off pieces of leaf and carry them back to their nest. They are very strong and can carry pieces of leaves many times their own size. Inside the nest, the ants use the leaves for food to eat.

Secretive snake

The emerald tree boa is hard to spot when it winds its leaf-green coils around branches and keeps quite still. This allows it to hide from enemies such as forest eagles and strike its prey without being seen.

Baby carrier

For the first year of its life a baby orangutan clings to its mother's fur and sleeps in the leafy nest she makes at night. As the baby grows up, its mother teaches it how to make its own nest, where to find food and how to climb and swing from tree to tree in the rainforest.

Big cat

Tigers are the biggest cats in the world. These fierce, strong hunters usually come out at night to catch food, such as deer or wild pigs. Tigers have to work hard for their meals because their prey can run fast or hide behind the forest trees and bushes. Often, a tiger will not catch anything to eat for a week!

Animal armour

Pangolins are covered in overlapping plates, which protect them like a suit of armour. They have no teeth, but use their long tongue to scoop up insects and swallow them whole.

Tree kangaroo

In the rainforests of Australia and New Guinea there are no monkeys and apes. Instead, tree kangaroos climb through the trees, clinging to the branches with the rough, non-slip soles on their feet. The kangaroo's long tail acts as a rudder when it leaps from branch to branch.

Treetop monkeys

Tiny squirrel monkeys leap along thin branches in the rainforest treetops, like the squirrels that live in cooler forests. They live in big groups, sometimes with several hundred monkeys in a group. During the day, they follow their leader through the trees, and at night they sleep huddled together on the branches.

Nosey tapir

The Malayan tapir uses its long nose to pull leaves and fruits from rainforest plants. Its sturdy, rounded body is a good shape for pushing its way through the undergrowth on the rainforest floor. Baby tapirs are well camouflaged from enemies by patterns of stripes and spots.

Bat transport

Fruit bats fly through the forest at night, feeding on flowers and fruits and helping to spread seeds and pollen. The flowers use strong scents to attract the bats, and mostly have pale colours that show up well in the dark.

Face paints

Male mandrills look as if they are wearing face paints! Females prefer males with brightly coloured faces. Mandrills live in large groups called troops, with a top male in charge. They search for food on the rainforest floor during the day and climb into the trees to sleep at night.

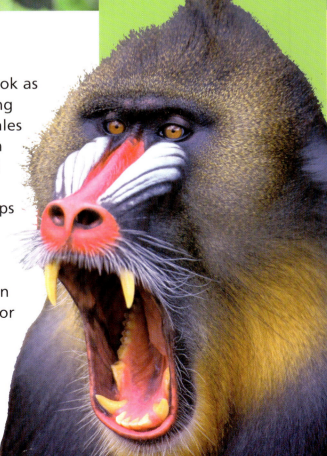

Grasslands

Grasslands grow in places where it is too dry for forests and too wet for deserts. There are two main kinds of grasslands – hot grasslands, such as the African savannah, and warm grasslands, such as the North American prairies, South American pampas grasslands and the Asian steppes.

On the move

To find enough food and water, wildebeest often wander over the grasslands on long journeys called migrations. They may cover thousands of kilometres each year. Wildebeest are noisy animals and are also called gnus, which is an African word for the snort that they sometimes make.

LOCATION

Climate
The prairie grasslands of North America receive between 50 and 90 cm of rainfall in a year

Habitat
Grasses are tough plants. If they are damaged by fire or drought, or eaten by grazing animals, they quickly sprout up again

Earthwatch
Many natural grasslands, such as the prairies, have been turned into farmland for growing crops or grazing farm animals

26

Hunting cat

Lions live in groups, called prides. The females, called lionesses, catch food and look after the cubs, while males protect the pride. By hunting together, lionesses can kill animals as large as zebras. They are powerful hunters with sharp teeth and claws.

Dog monkey

Baboons are monkeys with a long face rather like a dog. They even bark like dogs to warn of danger. They live mainly on the ground and walk on all fours. Babies cling to the fur on their mother's belly for the first few months, then ride on her back when they are about four months old.

Little and large

A baby elephant, or calf, stays close to its mother and drinks her milk until it is four to six years old. Other adults in an elephant family help too, by shading the calves from the sun and guarding them from predators while they sleep. Calves spend a lot of time playing together too!

Out of the way!

The word rhinoceros means 'horned nose', and rhinos scare their enemies by taking charge at them with these sharp horns. Rhinos have a very thick skin, which protects them from sharp thorns and bites from rivals or enemies. They usually live to around 50 years old.

Olympic sprinter

The cheetah is the fastest animal on land over short distances. It can reach 97 km/h in just three seconds! It can only run at top speed for about 60 seconds because it gets too hot. As a cheetah runs, its spiky claws grip the ground like the spikes on a sprinter's running shoes.

Skyscraper neck

A giraffe's extra-long neck allows it to feed on the highest leaves and twigs, up to 6 metres above the ground. Smaller grazing animals, such as zebras and gazelles, cannot reach this food. Giraffes use their long tongue and thick, rubbery lips to strip leaves from branches.

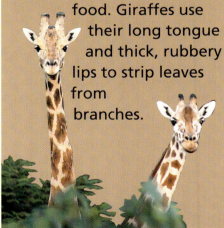

An ostrich's egg is so strong that an adult person can stand on one without breaking it

Elephants eat many different kinds of plants but most of their diet is grass. They feed for about 16 hours a day

A very thirsty adult elephant can drink about 98 litres of water in five minutes!

The money from tourists watching wildlife on safaris helps to preserve the African grasslands

Biggest bird

Ostriches are the biggest birds in the world – much taller than a person. Although they cannot fly, their long legs allow them to run away from danger at speeds of up to 70 km/h. Ostriches are nearly seven times too heavy to fly. Their long legs help them see over the tops of tall grasses and spot predators with their huge eyes.

Weaving experts

Male weaverbirds make complex hanging nests by weaving and knotting lots of strips of grass together. Males hang upside down from the finished nest, flicking their wings to attract a female. If the female likes the nest, she lays her eggs inside and raises the young by herself.

Recycling bird

On their long, wide wings, vultures float high in the sky keeping a sharp look out for animal bodies on the ground far below. By feeding on dead animals, vultures clean up the savannah grasslands and recycle the goodness in living things. A bare head and neck allows a vulture to feed without getting its feathers dirty.

Buzzy bee

As a bumblebee flaps its wings up and down, it makes a buzzing sound. Bumblebees have a hairy body, which keeps them warm. Strong hairs on the bee's back legs form a basket that the bee uses to collect pollen, a yellow dust found in flowers.

Long jumper

Grasshoppers have very long back legs. The big muscles at the top of these legs give them the power to make very long jumps through the grass. Jumping is quicker than walking, and helps the grasshoppers to escape danger. If a grasshopper is caught by one of its back legs, it can break off the leg to escape from an enemy.

Egg ball

Dung beetles feed on animal droppings, or dung. The adults shape pieces of dung into balls and roll them to a safe place, where they bury them in the ground. The female lays her eggs in the dung ball so the young will have plenty of food to eat when they hatch out of the eggs.

Hop to it

The kangaroo's long and heavy tail acts like a giant foot. It allows the kangaroo to balance, so he doesn't fall over when he hops. Baby kangaroos are called joeys, and they are no bigger than a peanut when they are born.

Deserts

Deserts are very dry places, where it is usually very hot by day and freezing cold at night. There are few large animals in deserts because there is not enough food and water to keep them alive. Smaller animals hide away in burrows during the day and come out at night, when it is cooler and damper.

Big ears

The fennec fox has huge ears, which work like radiators to give off heat and keep it cool. Big ears are also useful for tracking the sounds made by the fox's prey. The long hairs inside a fennec fox's ears keep out all the dust and sand.

Storage hump

A camel's hump is made up mostly of fat, which can be broken down to provide energy when food and water are hard to find. Dromedary camels, from Africa, have one hump, while Bactrian camels, from Asia, have two humps.

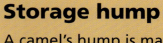

A camel can drink up to 50 litres of water in a few minutes

LOCATION

Climate
Deserts are places where there is usually less than 25 cm of rain a year. Some deserts see no rain at all for several years

Habitat
The Sahara Desert covers an area of North Africa almost as big as the USA. It is the largest desert in the world

Earthwatch
Some deserts are getting bigger, which may be linked to climate change or the problems caused by people, or for both reasons

Never thirsty

Kangaroo rats do not drink at all, but get all the moisture they need from their food. They are named after their long back legs, which look like those of a real kangaroo. Kangaroo rats use their long legs to jump out of reach of predators.

Winning races

The wild ass, or onager, can run as fast as a racehorse and goes on long journeys to find enough to eat and drink. It can survive for two or three days without drinking, which means it can survive in dry desert conditions.

Speedy rabbit

The jackrabbit bounds across the desert at speeds of up to 56 km/h on its powerful back legs, allowing it to escape from predators. It likes to come out in the cool of the night, and, like the fennec fox, has big ears to give off heat.

Desert traveller

Desert antelope often have to travel long distances in search of food and water. The wide hooves on their feet help spread out the weight of their body and stop them sinking into the sand. Desert antelope live in groups called herds. Both males and females have horns.

Modern desert towns use large amounts of energy and water, most of which has to be brought in from outside the desert

Deserts are not always hot, even in the daytime. It can be as cold as −34°C in Asia's Gobi Desert

Gila ('heela') monsters are endangered, large poisonous lizards that live in the deserts of North America

Only really hardy plants like the cactus can survive in the desert. When it rains, cacti can store loads of water

31

Honey jars

At rainy times, some honeypot ants store the sweet liquids from plants inside their bodies. They stay underground, and when food is hard to find, other ants feed from these living honeypots.

Shy runner

The roadrunner is a type of cuckoo that is often seen on desert roads. It is a shy bird that runs quickly away from danger at speeds of up to 24 km/h. Its long tail works like a brake or a rudder, and helps the bird stop suddenly or swerve in a different direction.

Keep away!

When a rattlesnake shakes the dry scales on its tail this makes a buzzing sound. The buzz tells predators, "Keep away! I have a poisonous bite and am very dangerous." Rattlesnakes use their poison, called venom, to kill their prey at cool times of the day.

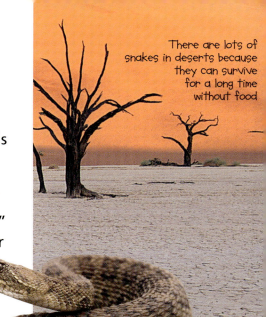

There are lots of snakes in deserts because they can survive for a long time without food

Flying flocks

Budgerigars fly over the Australian deserts in large flocks that may contain thousands of birds. These fast-flying parrots fly long distances in search of water. They avoid the hottest part of the day, feeding on seeds in the early morning or late afternoon, when it is cooler.

Wild budgerigars are mainly green and yellow, but people who breed them like to make them more colourful

Spiny protection

The cactus wren builds a large, dome-shaped nest in the middle of a spiny cactus. The parent wrens have tough feathers and hard, scaly legs, which prevents them from getting scratched on the cactus spines.

Cactus spines protect the baby birds from predators, like a spiked barbed-wire fence

Spiky lizard

The thorny devil lizard is covered in hard spines, which protect it from attack. To drink, it collects tiny drops of water on its skin in the night, which then run along grooves in its skin to its mouth. Thorny devil lizards feed on ants. They can eat several thousand of these insects at a time.

Hidey owl

The elf owl hides away in holes inside cacti to escape the heat of the sun. In the cool of the night, it comes out to feed, catching insects with its sharp talons. The elf owl is the smallest owl in the world. It is between 13 and 16 cm long, about the same size as a sparrow.

Islands

Islands such as the Galapagos, Madagascar and Australia are home to some very unusual animals. Many of them are unique, which means they are found only on one island and nowhere else in the world. Some island animals have grown into giants, while others are tiny. Rare island animals are often threatened by people, or by the animals people introduce to the islands.

Flightless bird
The kiwi of New Zealand cannot fly, and behaves more like a mammal than a bird. It comes out at night, sniffing for worms and insects with the sensitive nostrils at the end of its long bill. It is rare for a bird to have a good sense of smell.

Island giants
The Galapagos Islands are home to twelve kinds of giant tortoises. The word "Galapagos" is Spanish for a saddle that turns up at the front, like the shells of some of these tortoises. They grow up to 130 cm long and can weigh as much as three men. Giant tortoises may live for over 150 years.

LOCATION

 Climate
The Galapagos Islands are on the Equator where it is usually really hot, but cold water currents help keep it cool here

 Habitat
Madagascar is the world's fourth largest island. More than 80 per cent of the plants and animals on the island are unique

 Earthwatch
Since European settlers arrived in Australia about 200 years ago, they have cleared many forests

Big nose

The male proboscis monkey from the island of Borneo has a very large nose, which probably helps him attract females. Females have much smaller noses. Proboscis monkeys are very agile. They leap through mangrove trees, using their long tails to help them balance.

Baby pouch

Australia is home to many different mammals that rear their babies in pouches on the mother's body. A baby koala lives in its mother's pouch for six months until it is big and strong enough to be carried around on her back.

Alarm clock bird

Kookaburras are sometimes called the "bushman's clock" because their loud chuckling call wakes people up in the Australian bush at dawn. Kookaburras are giant kingfishers, but rarely eat fish. Instead, they catch snakes, small mammals and other birds.

Stripy tail

The ring-tailed lemur's stripy tail helps it balance. The male ring-tails rub their tails with scent from the glands on their bodies, and have "stink fights" with other males! Lifting their tails in the air signals to other lemurs.

Dreadful dragon

The Komodo dragon is the largest lizard in the world, growing up to 3 metres long. Although it is not a fire-breathing dragon, it is still a very dangerous reptile. It kills water buffalo with its sharp claws and a bite full of deadly bacteria.

 The tuataras that live on islands off the coast of New Zealand look similar to their relatives that lived with the dinosaurs

 The leaves of the eucalyptus trees that koalas eat do not give them much energy, so they spend most of their time asleep

 Two-thirds of the world's chameleons live on the island of Madagascar. Lemurs and birds called vangas live here too

 The marine iguana of the Galapagos Islands is the only lizard that swims and feeds in the sea. It holds its breath underwater

Coral reefs

Coral reefs are like the rainforests of the sea because they are full of such a variety of wildlife. They grow mainly in the shallow, clear water of tropical oceans where the coral animals have enough sunlight and warmth to survive. The warm waters are full of brightly coloured fish, sponges, sea anemones, worms, starfish and sea snakes.

Razor teeth

Moray eels hide in gaps between the coral, darting out to catch fish that swim nearby. They have long, razor-sharp teeth to grab their prey. Unlike most other moray eels, zebra moray eels have flat teeth for crushing the hard bodies of crabs, sea urchins and other prey.

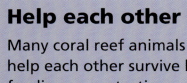

Help each other

Many coral reef animals help each other survive by feeding or protecting each other. The clown fish keeps safe by hiding among the stinging tentacles of sea anemones. It covers itself in slime for protection against the stings. The bright colours of the fish may warn predators of the anemones' dangerous tentacles, and therefore help keep both animals safe.

LOCATION

Climate
Coral reefs are very sensitive to changes in water temperature, and they take thousands of years to form

Habitat
A coral reef is made up of billions of little coral skeletons, piled on top of each other. Most are no bigger than your thumbnail

Earthwatch
Coral reefs are threatened by pollution, overfishing, drilling for oil and by the dumping of waste on top of the reef

Plant or animal?

Corals look rather like flowers, but they are really tiny animals related to sea anemones and jellyfish. Each coral animal, called a polyp, has a soft body and a ring of tentacles that wave in the water to trap particles of food. It grows a protective casing around its soft body. When the coral animals die, their empty casings build up to form a reef, on which new corals grow.

How many arms?

Do you know how many arms an octopus has? These arms are lined with suckers and are used for swimming, gripping prey and fighting. Octopuses have large eyes to help them find their prey, and sharp, beak-like jaws to bite and tear their food. They can change colour for camouflage, or as their mood changes.

Fish with a beak

Parrotfish have strong jaws that look rather like a parrot's beak. They use their strong 'beak' to scrape off little plants that are growing on the coral. Male parrotfish are more brightly coloured than the females.

Inflatable fish

If a porcupine fish is threatened, it quickly gulps down water or air, puffing up its body so it is too big for most predators to swallow. When the fish inflates its body, spines stick out of its skin, rather like the spiny quills of a porcupine.

Family colours

The bright colours and patterns of butterfly fish help them recognize other fish like themselves and attract a mate. Their long snouts help them reach into small holes in the reef to find food.

Heavyweight shell

The giant clam can measure up to 1.4 metres across, and its thick shell can weigh up to 180 kg. It feeds by filtering food from the water, and also absorbs some of the food made by tiny plants living in its fleshy 'lips'. The plants are protected by the clam – so plants and clam help each other to survive.

The Great Barrier Reef stretches for nearly 2,000 km off Australia. The biggest in the world, it can be seen from the Moon!

The lionfish is covered in lots of long, highly poisonous spines, which give would-be predators a very nasty sting

The largest predators on a coral reef are reef sharks, which patrol the deep water by the reef, looking for stray fish

The weedy sea dragon looks more like a piece of seaweed than a fish! Fleshy flaps cover its body, camouflaging it well

37

Oceans

Animals live at different levels in the oceans, from the sunlit waters on the surface to the darkest depths. Ocean temperatures are less extreme than on land, and the water supports the animals' bodies. Shoreline animals have to cope with dramatic change every day, because the seawater moves up and down the beach twice a day with the tides, and the waves also crash against the shore.

Stone tools

Sea otters crack open shellfish and sea urchins by bashing them against a stone. Then the otter is able to eat the soft flesh inside. Sea otters have thick, waterproof fur to keep them warm. An adult sea otter has hundreds of millions of hairs.

What's different?

True seals, such as grey seals, swim with their back flippers, while sea lions swim with their front flippers. Sea lions are better at moving on land than true seals. They can use their front flippers to push their bodies up off the ground, and turn their back flippers forwards to work like feet.

LOCATION

Climate
The wind creates strong currents on the ocean's surface, and these have an effect on the weather around the world

Habitat
The world has five oceans – the Pacific, Atlantic, Indian, Southern and Arctic Oceans. They are all linked together

Earthwatch
Many whales have been hunted almost to extinction. Controlling the hunting helps, but many are still threatened

Ocean giant

Humpback whales strain fish and small floating creatures from the seawater using fringed plates that hang down from their jaws like curtains. They have to come to the surface to breathe. They breathe by using a pair of blowholes on the top of their head.

Streamlined shape

A dolphin's body is a good shape for slipping easily through the water. It also has a smooth skin, with no hairs to slow it down while it swims. To move forwards, dolphins beat their tail flukes up and down. Their fins help them steer and change direction.

Fish holder

Puffins catch small fish underwater. They can hold twelve or more fish in their bill at once. Sharp edges to the bill and spines on the tongue stop the fish from sliding out. The puffin also uses its bill to dig a nesting burrow in a grassy cliff top.

Clever camouflage

An oystercatcher's eggs look like pebbles, so they are difficult for predators to spot on a pebbly beach. The male and female take turns sitting on the eggs, which hatch after about four weeks. The fluffy chicks can run around soon after hatching.

Washing line

A cormorant's feathers are not waterproof, unlike the feathers of most other waterbirds. After swimming underwater to catch fish, a cormorant holds out its wings to dry them. It pushes itself through the water with its webbed feet, reaching depths of about 10 metres.

Feed me

A herring gull chick pecks at a red spot on its parent's bill to make the parent cough up food. Herring gulls feed on fish out at sea and swallow the food to help them carry it for long distances. Herring gulls feed on rubbish dumps as well as out at sea.

Starfish usually have five arms, but may have between four and fifty arms!

Manta rays grow to 7 metres across, and weigh over 1,524 kg. They sometimes leap out of the water to escape predators

A female hawksbill turtle can lay over 250 eggs at one time! The eggs then take about 60 days to hatch

Sperm whales can stay underwater for more than two hours, hunting for giant squid and other prey

Baby beaches

Sea turtles, such as green turtles, spend most of their lives swimming through the oceans with their strong flippers. The females come ashore at night to lay their eggs on sandy beaches. Each female green turtle lays about 100 eggs at a time. She has to lay many eggs because most of her babies will not survive.

Borrowed home

Unlike most crabs, a hermit crab does not have a hard shell on the back part of its body. So, it borrows an empty shell to live in. The crab can hide inside the shell if it is attacked by a predator, such as a seabird. As it grows bigger, it swaps the shell for a larger one.

Plant or animal?

A sea anemone looks rather like a flower, but it is in fact an animal. It catches fish and other small sea creatures in its stinging tentacles. When the tide goes out, it pulls in its tentacles and fills its body with water so it looks like a blob of jelly. This stops it from drying out until the tide comes in and covers it with water again.

New arms for old

If one of a starfish's arms is damaged or bitten off, it can grow a new one. A starfish has to keep its body damp. At low tide, when the beach dries out, it hides underwater in rock pools or under rocks, where it is cool and moist.

Pouched horse

A female seahorse lays her eggs in a pouch on the front of the male's body. The male seahorse carries the developing babies around for a few weeks until they are ready to swim off and look after themselves. The baby seahorses suck up thousands of shrimp a day, and grow quickly.

Stinging jelly

Jellyfish sting small fish with their long trailing arms, called tentacles. The stings stop the fish from moving, so the jellyfish can use their frilly tentacles to pull the fish into their mouth. A jellyfish's mouth is in the middle of its bell-shaped body. Jellyfish are around 95 per cent water.

Razor teeth

The great white shark is a huge and powerful hunter that can swallow seals whole. Its razor-sharp teeth keep breaking off, but new teeth grow to replace them. A great white shark may use thousands of teeth in a lifetime.

Polar areas

In the frozen lands and oceans around the North Pole and the South Pole, animals have to survive bitterly cold temperatures, fierce winds and long, dark winters. Polar animals rely on thick fur, feathers or layers of fat to keep them warm. Many animals journey to polar regions for the short, warm summers, when there is plenty of food to eat and lots of safe nesting places.

Perfect penguins

Penguins cannot fly, but they are brilliant swimmers. They use their flippers to 'fly' underwater, and spend up to three-quarters of their lives in the sea. They come to land only to nest and rear their young. Large numbers of penguins nest together in huge, noisy colonies of as many as a million birds.

LOCATION

Climate
The average winter temperature in Antarctica is −60°C. Winds of up to 300 km/h cause blizzards and snowdrifts

Habitat
Antarctica is a vast frozen continent around the South Pole. It is one and a half times the size of the USA

Earthwatch
Some of the ice is melting in polar areas because of 'global warming,' or an increase in the Earth's average temperature

Summer bird

Every year, Arctic terns fly from one end of the world to the other and back again. This means they have one summer near the North Pole and then a second summer near the South Pole. They never have to survive cold winter weather and always have plenty of food and daylight.

Longest wings

The wandering albatross has the largest wingspan of any bird. It glides over the cold oceans in the southern part of the globe searching for food, and comes to land only to nest. Chicks stay in the nest for nearly a year, using their thick feathers and layers of fat to keep warm.

Great white bear

Polar bear cubs are born in a warm den, which their mother digs under the snow. The cubs are tiny and helpless at first, but they grow quickly as they feed on her rich milk. In just one year, the cubs are as big as a person. They stay with their mother for about two years while she teaches them how to hunt and survive.

Musical marks

Adult harp seals have black markings, which are shaped like a harp. Their pups are born on sheets of ice floating on the ocean, and have thick, fluffy white coats to keep them warm. The white colour also helps them blend into a background of white ice, making it harder for predators to spot them.

Helpful whales

Killer whales hunt in large groups called pods. This helps them catch larger prey than one whale could catch on its own. Killer whales catch seals and other large whales as well as fish and seabirds, including penguins.

Walrus warmth

Walruses have very thick layers of fat under their skin, which keep them warm in freezing oceans near the North Pole. Both males and females have long, pointed teeth called tusks, which they may use to fight each other, or for defence. Walruses use their fleshy noses and whiskers to feel for food on the seabed.

Most of Antarctica is covered by a sheet of ice, which in some places is as much as 4 km deep

Male emperor penguins do not eat for over 15 weeks while they keep an egg warm and wait for their chick to hatch

The icefish has a chemical in its blood that stops it freezing, like antifreeze stops water freezing in a car radiator

Polar areas are called 'Lands of the Midnight Sun' because in the summer it never gets dark and the Sun can shine all night

Summer holiday

Snow geese fly thousands of kilometres to spend the summer in cold northern regions. There they can nest and raise their young in places where there are few predators to disturb them. The snow geese have thick, fluffy feathers next to their skin to keep them warm in the freezing conditions.

Feather duvet

The female eider duck pulls out some of her own fluffy feathers to line her nest. This lining works like a feather duvet. It traps warm air near the eggs so they develop properly. The feathers also help hide the eggs from predators, such as foxes and gulls.

Distance runner

Wolverines hunt alone at night, chasing their prey for many kilometres without getting tired. These animals are very strong for their size and have a powerful bite. They can kill animals as big as reindeer.

Snowshoe feet

Arctic hares have big, furry feet, which allow them to move over the snow without sinking in very far. To escape from predators such as Arctic foxes, they can run very fast on their extra-long back legs.

Changing colour

The Arctic fox grows brown fur in summer and white fur in winter. This means that it always blends in with the background, and can creep up on its prey without being seen. It wraps its thick bushy tail around its body like a furry blanket to keep itself warm.

Polar ghost

Gliding silently over the ground, snowy owls swoop down to catch prey in their sharp talons. Snowy owls nest in a shallow dip in the ground, lined with moss or feathers. They do not lay all their eggs at once, so there is a mix of ages and sizes of chicks in their nest at the same time.

Christmas deer

Reindeer, or caribou, are the only deer in which both males and females grow antlers. Reindeer make long journeys north in the summer and then south again in the winter. The calves are born during the journey, and can run faster than a person when they are only one day old. They have to keep up with the adults to stay safe from predators.

Long hair

Musk oxen have very long fur coats to help them keep warm. The edges of their hooves are sharp enough to dig through snow and ice and reach food hidden underneath. If a group of musk oxen are attacked, they form a tight circle with the young in the middle. The adults defend the young with their big, curved horns.

45

Our habitat

Some wild animals live in our homes and gardens because there is plenty of food all year round and a variety of places to shelter and nest. During the winter, they may also move to our towns and cities where the weather is warmer than it is in the countryside. Many people also keep them as pets or farm animals.

Keeping bees

People build artificial nests, called hives, for honeybees to use. They can then harvest some of the wax that the bees produce to build their nest. Bees make honey from sweet flower nectar and store this in their nest to help them survive the winter. Beekeepers also take some of this honey for people to eat.

In some cities, there are as many rats as people! They live under our feet in sewers, drains and other underground tunnels

People first started to keep dogs as pets about 12,000 years ago. Cats only became pets about 4,000 years ago

In some European towns, white storks nest on chimneys instead of tall trees. They are believed to bring good fortune

Over 100 years ago, small flock of starling were released in New York. Today, there are over 50 million in North America

Popular pets

The most popular pets are cats, dogs, fish and budgerigars, but many children keep small pets such as hamsters, mice, gerbils, guinea pigs and rabbits. Keeping a pet is a good way to learn about animals. Any type of pet needs a lot of daily care and attention.

Keeping cows

Farmers keep cows mainly for their meat and milk, although leather can also be made from their skins. Cow horns can be used to make music or sound warnings, or made into things such as walking sticks, buttons and combs.

Milk is a good source of calcium. This helps our bones grow

Warning colours

Ladybirds are easy to spot in gardens and parks because of their bright red colour. This bright colour warns predators that ladybirds taste nasty, so they leave them alone. These much-loved insects are useful to people because they eat the greenflies that damage crops and garden plants. One ladybird can eat up to 50 greenflies a day.

Helpful horses

For thousands of years, people have tamed wild horses and used them for carrying loads, farming, racing and riding. Today, there are hundreds of different kinds of tame horses, from tiny Shetland ponies to huge shire horses. It is essential to groom a horse to keep its coat clean and in good condition.

Woolly fleeces

Most of our wool comes from the woolly coat that sheep grow, which is called a fleece. A sheep's fleece is cut off in spring or summer when the sheep does not need its thick woollen coat to keep warm. This is rather like having a haircut. It does not hurt the sheep, and the fleece soon grows back.

Butterfly plants

Plants that produce plenty of sweet nectar encourage butterflies, such as this peacock butterfly, to visit a garden. These plants include polyanthus, catmint, buddleia and honesty. Butterflies find buddleia bushes so attractive that they are called butterfly bushes.

In Australian cities, possums sometimes set up home in the attics of houses

In tropical countries, geckos are welcome in houses because they catch insects. Geckos have suction pads on their toes

About one million dust mites live in a single bed. They feed on the bits of dead skin that flake off our bodies

The world's fastest racehorses are able to run at up to 64 km/h over short distances

Town pigeons

Pigeons nest on rocks and cliffs in the wild, and are quite at home nesting on the artificial cliffs provided by the buildings in our towns and cities. People have kept pigeons for eating, for flying in races and for carrying messages tied to their feet.

Rascal raccoons

Like the red fox, the streetwise raccoon will eat almost anything. It thrives in towns and cities in North America, nesting in chimneys or drains instead of the hollow tree trunks it uses in the wild. In a city, a raccoon is safer from traps and hunters, which are a threat in the countryside.

House sparrows

These familiar birds are good at living near people, and have spread to most parts of the world. They usually stay close to buildings, often making their grassy nests in holes in walls. Female sparrows lay four or five eggs, which hatch in about two weeks. The young sparrows are ready to fly from the nest in about another two weeks.

Make it snappy

Alligators have lived in the wetlands of the US state of Florida for hundreds of years. The human population is growing in this area, and the number of alligator attacks on people, pets and farm animals in Florida has increased significantly since the year 2000.

Alligator warning street sign

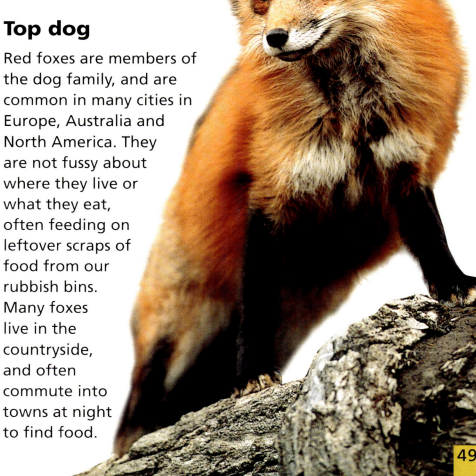

Motorway hunter

Kestrels often hover above the grassy edges of motorways, looking for mice and other prey moving through the grass below. They beat their wings very fast and spread out their tail to stay in one spot in the air for a long time. When the kestrel spots a meal, it slowly swoops down, grabbing the prey in its sharp claws.

Mouth sponge

Houseflies do not have a mouth with teeth, and can only digest liquid foods. To eat, first they spit onto their food to turn it into a sort of soup. Then they mop this up with the spongy pad on their head. A housefly also has rather unusual feet. They are able to taste its food!

Top dog

Red foxes are members of the dog family, and are common in many cities in Europe, Australia and North America. They are not fussy about where they live or what they eat, often feeding on leftover scraps of food from our rubbish bins. Many foxes live in the countryside, and often commute into towns at night to find food.

49

Animals in danger

Thousands of animals are endangered because people hunt or sell them, or destroy their habitats. Endangered animals include big animals such as Asian elephants, as well as small animals such as insects. To help endangered animals survive, we can find out more about how they live, protect their habitats, and control pollution and poaching (illegal hunting). We can also breed rare animals in captivity so they can be put back into the wild.

Night senses

There are about 1,600 giant pandas left in the bamboo forests and mountains of China, where they are protected in nature reserves. At present, these reserves are cut off from each other, but attempts are being made to link them. This would allow the pandas to move from one forest to another. Many pandas have been bred in captivity, and some have been released back into the wild to boost the numbers of pandas living there.

Mountain gorilla

There are only around 650 mountain gorillas left in the wild – in two separate areas of central Africa. Cutting down trees for farmland and timber is a threat to gorillas for two reasons. Firstly, it means that they are losing their habitat. Also, with the forests opened up, hunters are able to kill them more easily. One way to protect mountain gorillas is to let tourists pay to watch and photograph them. This money can then be used to protect them from hunters. Unfortunately, wars in the region make this difficult.

Golden lion tamarin

Named because of the bright orange mane around their faces, less than 100 golden lion tamarins were left in 1980 in the forests of Brazil. 98 per cent of their forest home had been destroyed, and many were captured for zoos. Conservation of the remaining forest, and putting some captive-bred tamarins back into the wild has rescued them from extinction.

Asian elephant

Asian elephants are in much greater danger than their African cousins. There are probably only between 28,000 and 44,000 Asian elephants left in the wild. These elephants are threatened by the growing numbers of people who farm the land where they once lived undisturbed.

Snow leopard

No one is sure how many snow leopards survive in the wild, because they live high in the mountains of central Asia and are very difficult to count and study. The main threat to their survival is farming. Herds of sheep and goats overgraze the mountain grasslands, leaving less food for the wild sheep – the snow leopard's main prey.

Bactrian camel

The two-humped Bactrian camel has thick, dark fur, which keeps it warm in the cold deserts of Asia. Fewer than 1,000 of these camels survive in the wild. This is due to hunting and pollution, and is also because their habitat is being destroyed by mining and gas pipe laying. Two nature reserves have been set up to protect them.

Tiger

Over the last 100 years, tiger numbers have fallen drastically. The South China tiger is the most endangered tiger. There are only around 30 of these animals left. All tigers are threatened by people who poach for their body parts, such as their bones, skin and internal organs. These parts are used in some traditional medicines. Cutting down plants also damages their habitat.

Hyacinth macaw

The deep blue hyacinth macaw is the largest kind of macaw, which is a type of parrot. Thousands of these stunning birds have been captured and sold as pets. To capture them, people cut down trees to remove the young macaws from their nest holes. This destroys the nest site for future generations, and also destroys their habitat. The illegal trade in pet macaws must be controlled, their habitats protected, and birds bred in captivity released into the wild.

Yangtze River dolphin

The rarest of all the whales, dolphins and porpoises, it is more than likely that the Yangtze River dolphin is now extinct. There were once thousands of these unusual dolphins living in the Yangtze River in China, but scientists could not find any in 2006. They have been affected by pollution, the noise from boats, and over-fishing.

Leatherback turtle

The leatherback turtle is the biggest turtle alive today, and it is critically endangered. In some places, nesting females are killed for their meat, and their eggs are taken for food. Out at sea, the adult turtles often get trapped in fishing gear. This means they are unable to swim to the surface to breathe, and they drown under the water. Patrolling beaches helps prevent poaching, and can allow baby turtles to reach the sea safely.

Blue whale

Blue whales were killed in huge numbers in the first half of the twentieth century, and their bodies were used to make oil. They were hunted almost to extinction until 1966, when hunting was banned all over the world. Once, there could have been up to 350,000 blue whales swimming in the oceans.

Black rhino

In the early twentieth century, there were about 100,000 black rhinos living over most of Africa. Now there are only about 2,700. Their horns are made into dagger handles, and are ground up for use in traditional Asian medicines. Today, most black rhinos only manage to survive in south and east Africa in nature reserves, where they are protected by armed guards.

Amazing animals

From the biggest animal in the world to one that can paralyse ten people with its poison, these four pages are stuffed full of amazing facts about animals that break all sorts of records. You'll find out some incredible things about their weird diets, special senses, extraordinary eggs, as well as how they survive in extreme habitats.

The biggest bears live on Kodiak Island in Alaska. Kodiak bears may weigh as much as a small car

Size
The adult female blue whale is the largest animal in the world. The seawater supports her huge body, which can reach over 30 metres long, and can weigh more than 150 tonnes.

FACT The biggest fish are the whale shark and the basking shark. They grow up to 12 metres long, and feed on tiny plankton in the sea

FACT The goliath beetle is the heaviest insect. It weighs up to 100 grams — that is nearly as heavy as an apple!

FACT The smallest bird in the world is the bee hummingbird, at only 6 cm long. Of all birds, these have the fewest feathers

FACT The giraffe is the tallest animal in the world. Its neck grows up to 2.4 metres long. Giraffes can weigh as much as 1,400 kg

Speed
The fastest animal in the world is the peregrine falcon. To catch its prey, first it soars to a great height, then it drops very steeply through the air at super speeds of up to 200 km/h.

FACT An ostrich can cover up to 100 metres in just five seconds. That's about twice as quick as the fastest human sprinter!

FACT The three-toed sloth is the slowest mammal, moving along the ground at speeds of only 2 metres a minute

FACT The fastest fish in the sea is the sailfish. It can zoom through the water at speeds of over 100 km/h

FACT Dragonflies can fly at over 30 km/h. Amazingly, they can also hover, go backwards and forwards, and come to an instant stop

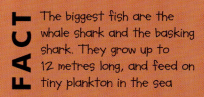

Senses

Sharks have an excellent sense of smell. They can detect the scent of blood from injured prey up to 500 metres away. They also have very sharp hearing, and these two senses combined make them ferocious hunters!

FACT Most spiders have eight eyes, but their eyesight is poor. They rely mainly on scent and vibrations to find out about their surroundings

FACT The male emperor moth can smell the special courtship scents that female emperor moths give off from around 11 km away

FACT Some long-eared bats have ears almost as long as their bodies. These help them detect tiny midges up to 20 metres away

FACT A bird's eyes are often as big as its brain. An ostrich's eyes are bigger than its brain. Ostriches have the largest eyes of any bird

Defence

The front horn of a white rhino can grow to be twice as long as a person's arm. Amazingly, it is made of hairs packed really tightly together – there's no bone in the middle of the horn.

FACT The front claws of a Kodiak brown bear can grow as long as a person's hand. The bears use these claws mainly for digging

FACT Caribou reindeer have really big antlers. They can grow to be more than 1.5 metres long

FACT Some butterflies and moths hide from predators by looking like leaves, twigs or even bird droppings

FACT Bombardier beetles squirt a boiling hot spray of poisonous chemicals at their attackers. They can spray this in any direction they wish

Survival

In order to survive extremely cold winters, marmots (also known as prairie dogs) hibernate in their burrows for as long as 10 months.

FACT Some mice can survive in meat cold-stores, where the temperature can sometimes fall below −9°C

FACT Camels don't sweat until their bodies reach 40°C. When they find water, they can drink 100 litres in just 10 minutes!

FACT In the desert, the male sand grouse flies up to 80 km in search of water. He carries the water back to his chicks in his chest feathers

FACT The highest living mammals are the yaks of the Himalayas. They climb as high as 6,100 metres, and endure temperatures of −40°C

Poisonous

Nearly all spiders use poison to kill or paralyse their prey, or to defend themselves. The Brazilian wandering spider has poison strong enough to kill 225 mice. Its bite has killed several people.

FACT One blue-ringed octopus can paralyse up to ten people with its poison. It has bright blue rings on its body to warn that it is deadly

FACT Only female wasps are able to sting. This is because the sting is made from the egg-laying tube, which only females have

FACT Giant centipedes with poisonous claws live in the American rainforests. These centipedes can grow up to 30 cm long

FACT Less than a quarter of all snakes are poisonous. The most poisonous snake in the world is the black-headed sea snake

Wings and limbs

The Australian sugar glider has flaps of skin along the sides of its body, which work like wings. The sugar glider can glide for more than 50 metres when moving between trees.

FACT A hummingbird beats its wings up to 75 times a second. It is this amazingly fast wing beating that produces the humming sound

FACT The male quetzal is a shiny green bird from Central America. His tail is more than twice the length of his body, and helps him attract a mate

FACT The African jacana has the longest toes of any bird. They help spread out its weight, so it is able to walk across swampy ground

FACT The wandering albatross has the biggest wingspan of any bird. It measures more than 3 metres from one wingtip to the other

Teeth and beaks

An elephant's tusks act as its front teeth. They grow at a rate of around 17 cm a year. A male's tusks can weigh up to 60 kg. Elephant tusks are made of a hard material called ivory.

FACT The longest fangs of any snake belong to the gaboon viper. These can grow up to almost 5 cm long

FACT The Australian pelican has the longest bill in the world. Male pelican bills can grow up to 47 cm long

FACT The wrybill of New Zealand is the only bird with a bill that curves to the right rather than to the left, but no one knows why this is!

FACT The hawfinch has the most powerful bill of any bird. It can easily crack cherry stones with this bill

Eggs and nests

Some tiny insects called termites build huge mud towers. These can be over 8 metres high. It takes termites between 10 and 20 years to build these incredible homes, and each home shelters millions of termites.

FACT The female grey partridge lays the most eggs at one time of any bird. She can lay up to 20!

FACT Only a few mammals, such as the platypus and the spiny anteater, lay eggs instead of giving birth to babies

FACT The biggest birds' nest is built by the bald eagle. One nest can weigh 2,000 kg – about the same as two army jeeps

FACT The nests of African sociable weaver birds look like the thatched roof of a cottage. As many as 300 birds can live in one nest

Babies

A newborn baby elephant weighs more than an adult human. Baby elephants feed on their mother's milk for up to six years. A female elephant has a really long pregnancy, lasting for 22 months.

FACT A baby blue whale weighs about 2.5 tonnes when it is born. That's hundreds of times heavier than a human baby weighs at birth

FACT Mother crocodiles carry their babies in their mouth to take them from their nest to the water. They can carry up to 20 babies at a time

FACT Anacondas give birth to live young, instead of laying eggs. The newborn anacondas are only 6 cm long, but can grow up to be over 6 metres!

FACT When it is born, a baby kangaroo, called a joey, is so small that it would fit into a teaspoon!

Food
Giant anteaters mainly eat ants and termites. Their tongues are about 60 cm long, and they use this long, sticky tongue to lick up as many as 30,000 of these tiny insects a day.

FACT An egg-eating snake can unhinge its jaws. This allows it to swallow eggs twice the size of its own head!

FACT Vampire bats are the only mammals that feed just on blood. They lap up blood from their prey, rather than sucking it

FACT Saltwater crocodiles can catch and kill really big animals like zebras and cattle. They can survive up to two years between meals

FACT A chameleon can stick out its long tongue to almost twice the length of its body. It catches insects on the tongue's swollen, sticky tip

Lifespan
The lifespan of an animal is the length of time for which it lives. Some animals live much longer than humans, while others have really short lives. Generally, the larger an animal is, the longer it tends to live.

Arctic clam – 220 years
Giant tortoise – over 200 years
Crocodile – up to 100 years
Killer whale – 90 years
Elephant – up to 70 years
Parrot – 50–80 years
Whale shark – 60 years
American lobster – 50 years
Hippopotamus – 45 years
Tiger – 22 years
Goldfish – 10–25 years
Goat – 15 years
Fox – 14 years
Platypus – 10 years
Toucan – 6 years
Rabbit – 6–8 years
Hamster – 3–4 years
Common shrew – 1 year
Housefly – 2–4 weeks
Mayfly – 3 hours

A baby gorilla is not strong enough to walk by itself until it is at least two and a half years old. It rides on its mother's back until then

Glossary

Acid rain
A type of rain that is formed when certain gases are released into the air and mix with water vapour. Acid rain damages trees and kills fish when it gets into rivers and lakes.

Camouflage
Features or patterns that make plants and animals look like their surroundings. Camouflage is useful because it allows plants and animals to hide from their enemies.

Captivity
When an animal is not free to roam wild, but is kept by people in a zoo or some other place that it is unable to leave of its own accord.

Colony
A group of animals belonging to the same **species**, that live together in a group. Many birds, for example penguins, live together in colonies.

Coniferous
A type of tree with thin leaves that produces cones, for example, pine trees. Coniferous trees are usually **evergreen**.

Continent
One of the main areas of land on Earth. There are seven continents in total. These are Europe, Asia, Africa, North America, South America, Australia and Antarctica.

Coral reef
A structure in the sea made up of the skeletons of tiny sea animals called polyps. Over many years a coral reef builds up as old polyps die and new ones grow on top of them.

Current
Currents are moving streams of sea water both on and below the surface. On the sea's surface they are caused by the wind. Currents affect weather systems around the world.

Deciduous
A type of tree that sheds its leaves each autumn. Most trees are deciduous. If a tree is not deciduous it is called **evergreen**.

Drought
A long period of dry weather, when very little, or no, rain falls. This makes it hard for crops to survive.

Endangered
To be threatened by something. An endangered animal is usually an animal threatened by **extinction**. Endangered animals are often kept in **captivity**.

Environment
The environment is a word used to describe everything that surrounds us on Earth. Earth's environment is unique. It is made up of air, water, and the heat and light from the Sun. Sometimes when people talk about the environment they are referring to the condition of the Earth, and to problems such as **global warming**.

Evergreen
A type of tree that does not lose its leaves in the autumn, but keeps them throughout the year. If a tree is not evergreen it is called **deciduous**.

Extinction
The process of dying out. Animals that become extinct, such as dinosaurs, no longer exist. If an animal is **endangered**, often this means that it is threatened by extinction.

Global warming
An increase in temperature throughout the world. This is most likely due to the greenhouse effect, which is when heat becomes trapped in the Earth's atmosphere. Global warming leads to changes in weather conditions.

Habitat
The place where a particular animal or plant is usually found. Often an animal or plant will live in a certain habitat because several things about it suit them, such as the type of soil, temperature or amount of light.

Herd
A group of animals belonging to the same species that stick together in a large group.

Hibernation
A sleep-like state that some animals enter in order to survive cold winter months. When in hibernation, their body temperature, heart rate and breathing rate all drop. The animals are able to remain totally inactive for long periods of time, but stay alive.

Migration
The move that some animals make, usually in large groups, from one place to another. Animals often migrate in order to find food, warm weather, or to breed.

Nectar
The sweet juice of a plant, which often attracts insects or birds.

Pollen
Powdery substance made by plants that is carried by wind and insects to other plants to fertilise them.

Pollution
When harmful substances are released into the **environment**. Many different types of substances can cause environmental pollution.

Population
The total number of people or animals that live in a particular area or **habitat**.

Predator
An animal that captures, kills, and eats other animals. The animal that is caught by a predator is called the **prey**.

Prey
An animal hunted by another animal for food. The animal that hunts prey is called the **predator**.

Recycle
To treat materials in a certain way that makes them suitable to be used again. Many different materials can be recycled, such as glass, plastic, metal and paper.

Safari
A journey or adventure, often in Africa, and usually to find animals.

Species
A group of animals or plants that share the same characteristics. This means they may look similar, or behave in similar ways.

Venom
The poisonous fluid that some animals, such as snakes and spiders, release into their victims when they bite or sting. Venom is another word for poison.

Wingspan
The length of a bird's wings, from the tip of one wing to the tip of the other.

Web directory

If you want to discover more about the animals in this book and many more fascinating facts, then here is our pick of the best animal sites on the web.

www.nationalgeographic.com/kids
Discover fun facts, listen to animal sounds and download postcards and photographs of wild animals.

www.kidsgowild.com/kidsgowild/animalfacts
Wildlife news and conservation information on everything from aardvarks to zebras.

www.bbc.co.uk/nature/reallywild/amazing
Follow this A to Z guide to the world and meet some of the most amazing animals on each continent.

www.kidsplanet.org/factsheets/map.html
Factsheets with information on over 50 endangered animals from all over the world.

www.allaboutnature.com/biomes
Information about the animals that live in the Earth's many habitats, from deserts and grasslands to forests and ponds.

dsc.discovery.com/guides/animals/animals.html
Read the latest news about animals, explore the oceans and discover which animals would win an 'animal Olympics.'

www.wwf.org.uk/gowild
Includes sections on animals, habitats, games, cool stuff and how you can help to save the world's rare animals.

www.animalinfo.org
Information about endangered mammals and links to animal-related sites, organisations and publications.

www.seaworld.org/animal-info/animal-bytes
Factsheets with information about the conservation, ecology, classification and physical features of hundreds of animals.

Index

A
Acid rain   16
Albatross   43, 56
Alligator   13, 49
Ant
    army ant   21
    honeypot ant   32
    leafcutter ant   23
Anteater   56, 57
Antelope   31
Ass   31

B
Bat
    fruit bat   25
    long-eared bat   17, 55
    vampire bat   57
Bear
    American black bear   17
    Kodiak bear   54, 55
    polar bear   43
Beaver   13
Bee   28, 46
Beetle
    bombardier beetle   55
    dung beetle   29
    goliath beetle   54
    stag beetle   19
Blue jay   19
Bushbaby   20
Butterfly   55
    monarch butterfly   19
    morpho butterfly   22
    peacock butterfly   47
Butterfly fish   37

C
Cactus   31, 32
Cactus wren   32
Camel   30, 51, 55
Cat (domestic)   46
Centipede   55
Chamois   11
Cheetah   27
Chimpanzee   21
Chinchilla   11
Clam   37, 57
Clown fish   36
Condor   11
Cormorant   39
Cow   47
Crab   40
Crocodile   14, 56, 57
Crossbill   18
Cuckoo   19, 32

D
Deer
    elk   16
    fallow deer   17
    moose   16
    reindeer   45, 55
Dog   46
Dolphin   39, 52
Dormouse   17
Duck   14, 44

E
Eagle   11, 56
Eel   36
Elephant   27, 51, 56, 57

F
Falcon   54
Flamingo   15
Fly
    dragonfly   14, 54
    greenfly   47
    housefly   49, 57
    mayfly   57
Fox   57
    Arctic fox   45
    fennec fox   30
    red fox   49

G
Gibbon   21
Giraffe   27, 54
Global warming   42
Goat   11, 57
Golden lion tamarin   51
Goldfish   57
Gorilla   51
Grasshopper   28

H
Hamster   57
Hare   45
Hawfinch   56
Heron   14
Herring gull   39
Hippopotamus   13, 57
Horse   12, 47
Hummingbird   54, 56

I
Icefish   43

J
Jacana   56
Jackrabbit   31
Jaguar   20
Jellyfish   41

K
Kangaroo   25, 29, 56
Kestrel   49
Kingfisher   14
kookaburra   35
Kiwi   34
Koala   35

L
Ladybird   47
Lemur   35
Lion   27
Lionfish   37
Lizard
    chameleon   35, 57
    devil lizard   33
    gecko   47
    gila monster   31
    green iguana   22
    Komodo dragon   35
    marine iguana   35
Lobster   57

M
Manatee   13
Mandrill   25
Mallard   14
Manta ray   39
Marmot   55
Medicine   21, 52, 53
Mite   47
Monkey
    baboon   27
    Japanese macaque   10
    proboscis monkey   35
    spider monkey   21
    squirrel monkey   25
    tarsier monkey   21
Moth   55
Mouse   55
Mudskipper fish   15
Musk ox   45

N
Nutcracker	17

O
Octopus	37, 55
Orangutan	24
Ostrich	27, 28, 54, 55
Otter	13, 38
Owl	
elf owl	33
snowy owl	45
tawny owl	18
Oystercatcher	39

P
Panda	11, 50
Pangolin	24
Parrot	57
budgerigar	32
hyacinth macaw	52
scarlet macaw	22
Parrotfish	37
Partridge	56
Pelican	56
Penguin	42, 43
Pigeon	48
Pine tree	16
Platypus	13, 56, 57
Polyp	37
Porcupine	16
Porcupine fish	37
Possum	47
Puffin	39

Q
Quetzal	56

R
Rabbit	57
Raccoon	48
Rat	46, 31
Rhinoceros	27
black rhinoceros	53
white rhinoceros	55

S
Safari	27
Sailfish	54
Sand grouse	55
Sea anemone	36, 40
Sea dragon	37
Seahorse	40
Seal	38, 43
Sea lion	38
Shark	55
basking shark	54
great white shark	41
reef shark	37
whale shark	54, 57
Sheep	47
Shrew	57
Sloth	21, 54
Snake	57
anaconda	56
black-headed sea	55
emerald tree boa	23
gabon viper	56
rattlesnake	32
Snow goose	44
Snow leopard	10, 11, 51
Sparrow	48
Spider	55
Brazilian spider	55
goliath tarantula	21
Squirrel	17
Starfish	39, 40
Starling	46
Stork	46
Sugar glider	56

T
Tapir	25
Termite	21, 56
Tern	43
Tiger	24, 52, 57
Tortoise	34, 57
Toucan	22, 57
Tuatara	35
Turtle	
green turtle	40
hawksbill turtle	39
leatherback turtle	53

V
Vulture	28

W
Walrus	43
Wasp	55
Weaverbird	28, 56
Whale	38
blue whale	53, 54, 56
humpback whale	39
killer whale	43, 57
sperm whale	39
Whip-poor-will	19
Wildebeest	26
Wolf	17
Wolverine	45
Woodpecker	18
Wrybill	56

Y
Yak	11, 55

Credits

Picture credits

A.N.T. Photo Library/NHPA: honeypot ant, page 32.

A.N.T. Photo Library/NHPA: sugar glider, page 56.

Arco Images/Alamy: spider monkey, page 21.

Arco Images/Alamy: crossbill, page 18.

Bob Elsdale/ The Image Bank/ Getty Images: dormouse, page 17.

David Fleetham/Alamy: blue whale, page 54.

Ellen McKnight/Alamy: leatherback turtle, page 53.

Fabrice Bettex/Alamy: great white shark, page 41.

Images and Stories/Alamy: proboscis monkey, page 35.

John Altringham: long-eared bat, page 17.

Jon Arnold Images/Alamy: kiwi, page 34.

Mark Carwardine/ NHPA: Yangtze River dolphin, page 52.

Mary McDonald/ Nature Picture Library: kangaroo rat, page 31.

Nicole Duplaix/National Geographic/ Getty Images: platypus, page 13.

Pete Oxford/ Robert Harding: pangolin, page 24.

Rick and Nora Bowers/Alamy: elf owl, page 33.